The Professional Organizer's Complete Business Guide

Copyright © 2006
by Lisa Steinbacher, Organize My Life!

Published by
Eternity Publishing
Kansas U.S.A.

Library of Congress Control Number: 2004093007
ISBN Number: 1-4116-0915-8

Contributions: Edited By Gregory P. Steinbacher

All rights reserved.

No part of this publication may be reproduced or utilized in any form or by any means electronic or mechanical, including photocopying, recording or by any information storage or retrieval system now known or hereafter invented, without the prior written permission of the Publishers. Any documents and/or forms provided on electronic media may be customized for personal use. However, any book text included on the electronic media (e-book text) may not be duplicated or used without express written consent of the publishers.

This publication is designed to provide accurate and informational details in regard to the subject matter herein. It is sold with the understanding that the copyright owner is not engaged in rendering legal, accounting or other professional service. If legal advice or other expert assistance is required, it is advised that an attorney be consulted or proper professional be sought.

While care has been exercised in the writing and compilation of this guide, the copyright owner, author, Publishers, their employees and agents, are not responsible for errors or omissions. This reference is intended to assist in providing information to the public, and the information is delivered and purchased by the purchaser with the understanding that it is the express personal opinion of the author who shall not be held liable under any circumstances for the contents contained herein. The Publishers and their respective employees or agents, as well as the author, editor and any employees or agents, assume no responsibility for injury or damage occasioned to any person as a result of participation in the activities described in this book, and make no warranty to the effectiveness of the techniques or examples given in this book. The purchaser of the book assumes all liability and responsibility.

For Greg,
because he married
a simple "uncluttered"
country girl,

and

For Mom,
because she taught me
the importance of
organization.

Table of Contents

1: In The Beginning.. 5
- Professional Organizer Defined 5
- Services Provided 5
- Skills, Experiences and Enjoyment Matter 6
- Credibility Matters 6
- Skills You Need 7
- How To Choose Your Specialty 8
- Certification 8

2: Getting Started 9
- Start-up Costs 9
- Supplies 9
- Business Cards, Brochures and Stationery 10
- Quitting Your Current Job 10
- Buying A Computer 11
- Advertising and Promotions 11
- Dress Code 11
- Licensing Your Business 13
- Naming Your Business 16
- Business Structure 17
- Federal Employer Identification Number (EIN) 22
- EIN Address and Phone Information* 23
- Financial Institutions and Bank Accounts 24
- External Funding and Loans 25

3: Money Matters 27
- What Income You Can Expect 27
- Quoting Your Project 27
- Hourly Rate 28
- Per Project Rate 28
- Small, Medium, and Large Rate Plan 28
- Estimating Project Completion Time 28
- Products Required For Project 29
- Deposit Requests 31
- The Nickel and Dime Syndrome 31
- Settling The Final Bill 31

4: Marketing 101 33
- Your Marketing Approach 33
- Create A Marketing Plan 33
- A Reality Check 34
- Your Marketing Strategy 34
- Cold Calls, Prospects and Customers 35
- Planting The Seed For Future Business 36

5: Marketing 201 37
- Your Target Audience 37
- Your Offer 37
- Making Your Offer Known 38
- Newspaper and Magazine Advertisements 40
- Phone Book Advertisements 41
- Church or Community Advertisements 41
- Web Site Advertisements 42
- Writing Your Own Articles 42
- Articles Written About You 43
- Advertising Flyers & Signs 43
- Direct Mail 43
- Doorknob Hangers 44
- Email Spam 44
- Newsletters 44
- News Releases 46

6: Generating Customers 47
- Getting Responses 47
- Your Follow Up 47
- Free Consultations 49
- The Appointment 49
- Assessing The Project 50
- Proposals 51
- Writing A Proposal 51
- Proposal Worksheet 52
- Project Proposal Terms and Conditions 53
- Turning Down A Job 54
- Guarantees 55

7: It Is All Business 56
- Customer Types 56
- Undesirable Situations 59
- Repeat Sales 59

Continuation Plans 60
Building Your Credentials 60
Conclusion 61

Chapter 1

1: In The Beginning...

Professional Organizer Defined

You are in a position as a skilled organizer to provide personal consulting, coaching, ideas, forms, seminars and products to help individuals and businesses get organized and continue with a planned system of organization!

SPECIALTIES
📁 Filing systems and workflow management
✏️ Financial/billing systems
💻 Computer consulting/office organizing
📖 Home/closet/space organizing and design

Professional Organizers have the option of specializing in a variety of different areas, as seen by a few of the possible specialties listed to the left. The most productive professionals specialize in a broad range of services, to meet all their customer's needs.

Services Provided

Professional organizers provide a wide range of services and products, such as:

- Personal consulting
- Hands-on organizing and design assistance
- Books, video, audio, newsletters, etc.
- Seminars and workshops
- Email, telephone, internet consulting
- Purchasing organizing products

Skills, Experiences and Enjoyment Matter

The services you provide to your customers should be based on your skills, experiences and your level of enjoyment. Any person who does a job they do not like will not be enthusiastic about the job or the service they are providing, and their lack of desire or energy will likely show to their customers. You should view organization as more of a hobby than a job, and you should always work to stay on top of current trends and information.

Credibility Matters

In order to gain the credibility you need to become successful, you should be willing to provide your customers with proof of your qualifications. The best way to do this is to create a portfolio of information about your past experiences. Education, workshop certificates, testimonials, photographs and notes from completed projects, are all things you can include in your portfolio to add to your credibility.

You have to know exactly how to help your customers. Know your business inside and out. Your clients expect you to be the expert, and to help them solve their organizing problems.

On occasion, prospective customers may ask for your credentials, or ask to see pictures of previous jobs you have done. Be prepared to sell yourself, and tell them what they need to know to feel comfortable in hiring you to do the job. It is imperative that you prepare for your initial meeting with a customer, like you are attending a job interview. You should prepare yourself to answer the inevitable question: "What qualifies you to be a professional organizer?" Know how you will answer this question, and be prepared to back it up with proof from your portfolio.

Try this: If you have never charged anyone a fee for your organizing services, but are ready to become a professional organizer, you need to gain some hands-on experience from somewhere. One of the best ways to get your name and skills known in public is to perform "no-fee" work for your friends, relatives, and acquaintances. Aside from gaining experience that you can use as credentials, you should always take "before" and "after" pictures of your work, no matter how small or large the project. You can also ask your customers (or friends and relatives in this case) to write a letter of recommendation, or a testimonial. Some people are hesitant to write testimonials on their own. In that case, I have included a *Customer Survey – Quality Scale* (Appendix A, Form 30) and a *Customer Survey – Testimonial* (Appendix A, Form 31) that you can give your customers and ask them to complete. This will help you improve your services and gain a perspective on their satisfaction level, and allows you to use the information in your testimonials.

Questions You Need Answers To: Some popular questions your customers may ask you that you need to be prepared to answer are:

- Are you an organized person? Do you specialize in any areas?

- How many customers do you have? Do you have repeat customers?

- How many hours of organization have you completed? How many hours of extra education or seminars have you attended?

- Have you created any organization products? Do you tend to use one particular brand of products more than others?

- Do you have a website or email address? Do you have a newsletter or booklet of organizational tips or ideas?

- Are you a member of NAPO or some other organization such as the Better Business Bureau?

- What kinds of projects have you worked on? What was the success and time frame of completion for the project?

- Do you have any testimonials, pictures, or former clients I may contact?

Skills You Need

Many professional organizers are already very organized individuals. Aside from being a talented organizer, it is important that you have a certain level of expertise in the area you want to be working in. For example, if you are planning on specializing in creating effective filing systems, you must know all about effective filing systems. You have to start with an idea, and work from there. You have to know the essentials, and all the products that go along with it, as well as the time management that is required to keep the system working.

Read everything you can get your hands on about organizing. Sign up for as many newsletters as you can find so you stay abreast of the current industry standards. Attend as many workshops and seminars as you can – especially in the beginning – so you can get a fresh perspective on other peoples ideas and organizing tips. Seek a mentor – someone who already has a successful business. Ask them if you can be a temporary "Intern" and do some work for free to gain some experience and learn from their expertise. (Note that some professional organizers in your area may not be open to this, as they do not want to train their future competition.)

Something you should never do in the beginning is practice on a paying customer. Your first few jobs should always be on an intern basis or complimentary work for relatives or friends. Avoid putting your business relationships on the line until you are sure of your skills and ability to handle a paying job with grace, ease and perfection.

How To Choose Your Specialty

Your business will be able to cater to a wider audience if you offer a wide range of services in which you specialize. On the opposite side of the coin, many professional organizers find it less stressful to narrow their specialty to a few key areas of expertise. I recommend offering the services that you are most comfortable with in the beginning, and as your business grows, you may settle in to your niche naturally by weeding out undesirable tasks.

If your customers are looking for someone to help them manage their time, classifying yourself as a "time management expert" is a great deal stronger than simply saying you "help to organize time, offices and homes."

Know that whatever you decide, it doesn't have to be written in stone immediately. You can develop and change your specialty as you desire or the need arises. The most important thing to remember is in order for you to be an effective and efficient professional organizer; you have to be good at what you do.

Certification

You do not need special certification in order to be a professional organizer. However, there are organizations that are excellent in providing information specific to the industry of organizing. The most popular, and by far, the most affordable is the Global Alliance of Professional Organizers (or "Global APO"). Global APO not only allows you to network with other professionals in the industry, but it also aids you in obtaining and maintaining professional credibility.

Think of Global APO as the "Better Business Bureau" of Organizing. It maintains a database of professionals, including information on whether or not a business or individual has had any complaints from customers regarding their service. Membership is affordable, (compared to other organizations, membership fees are at least half the cost) and you can pay monthly or yearly.

Members can specify the information they want displayed online, which is linked to their name in the directory. Global APO also awards a member certificate and laminated membership card each year – all which contribute to your professional credibility. Global APO has a special "members only" section, which contains hundreds of templates that you can download for free, and customize to suit your needs. It includes everything from marketing materials to contracts.

You can read more about the Global Alliance of Professional Organizers and sign up for membership at www.globalapo.com.

Chapter 2

2: Getting Started

Start-up Costs

Good news! The start-up cost for becoming a professional organizer is very low! As a matter of fact, something you shouldn't do when starting your business is to invest a lot of money up front. Eventually, you may have to spend some money for your business to be successful, but in the beginning, it is best to take it easy and lay low financially.

You may be wondering, "Do I need an office space?" My answer is "No." You can do this business right out of your home. Again, let me reiterate...lay low financially for a while. Most professional organizers work out of their home, and you may even qualify for tax breaks by doing it this way! Clients understand that this line of business is typically a sole proprietorship, and like the more personal one-on-one service they get. If your business grows, and you hire assistants and have the need for a secretary, or other employees, then it is advisable for you to obtain an office space outside of your home, as you have outgrown your home-office space.

Supplies

One of the first mistakes that new professional organizers make is to run out and buy all kinds of supplies that take their start-up costs higher than anticipated. Do not make this mistake! Wait – be patient. Eventually, you will acquire all the supplies you may ever need...but for now, while you're just starting up, keep it simple. You should not run out to a discount warehouse or office supply store and buy them out of file folders and blank invoice pads. Once you get your first client, there are a few things you may want to have, which are listed below. Anything that is not on the list can be found in Appendix A (forms, proposals, invoices, calendars, etc.) or can be purchased after you find you have a need for it, to complete whatever project you are working on.

Here is a basic list of supplies you should have for your first consultation:

- Business cards
- Measuring tape and camera
- Pens and pencils
- Notepaper and forms from Appendix A

Anything that is not included on this list is something you can purchase as the need arises for them. Remember to be conservative; keep it simple and inexpensive.

Business Cards, Brochures and Stationery

It is very easy to allow yourself to get wrapped up in little details like business cards, brochures and stationery. I recommend spending some time creating a brochure and business cards. They are relatively easy to create on a home computer, and your prospects will have a visual aid to help them understand your services, and the importance of getting organized.

I would like to make a small note about a company logo. Do not spend a great deal of time trying to come up with a logo, and above all, do not spend any money having a professional design one for you. For small businesses, logos do not do much to increase your profitability. Keep in mind that simple is usually elegant, and makes a great statement. Your name alone states that you are a personal consultant…a professional, and that is enough to make a good impression.

Full-page samples of brochures can be found in Appendix A, Forms 9 to 13. Business cards can be found in Appendix A, Forms 14 to 20. Customizable templates may be found on the companion *Forms CD* with the same form numbers and file names.

Quitting Your Current Job

If you are currently working another job, and your sole income is from that job, you should not "chuck it" and quit your job until your business is successful enough to support you by itself. It will take some time to get your business up and running, and if you do not have something to fall back on during slow times, in the beginning, your pocketbook may suffer. If your spouse is working a full time job and makes enough to financially support your family on his or her own, and he or she agrees; you may consider quitting your present job to focus all of your attention on building your business rather than trying to establish it on a part-time basis. A word of caution: make sure this is what you want to do before you quit your job. Be absolutely positive that you are going to dedicate your time and efforts to making this business successful. It would be very upsetting for you to quit your job, then get tired of being a professional organizer and quit after a short time, only to discover that you cannot return to your previous employment.

I do not want to discourage you from beginning your own professional organizer business, but at the same time, I do not want to sugar coat it so you forget the reality of the situation. Starting up a business of your own takes a great deal of work, effort, commitment, and time. You will endure times of emotional ups and downs while getting your business up and running. You have to be willing to endure the tough times to make it work. Give your all, or give nothing at all.

Buying A Computer

I highly recommend that you have a personal home computer. It is an indispensable tool for your business, both in helping you complete projects as well as in creating forms and documents, and tracking your income and expenses. You should also have Internet capabilities so you can do online research. You may also find great deals on supplies from online wholesalers that local merchants cannot match. If you are serious about becoming a professional organizer, your computer will become your lifeline. I have three computers, and consider myself to be a "self-taught computer junkie." You do not need extensive experience to be able to use a computer either, and there are so many options out there for first-time users to become more acquainted with their equipment. Ideally, you already have a personal computer that you can utilize, but if you do not, you should consider buying one. The costs of computers are going down, and the memory and capabilities are going up – so if you are serious, please consider it as a valuable tool.

Advertising and Promotions

A common mistake new professional organizers make is to invest a considerable amount of money in newspaper ads, yellow page ads, and other types of advertisements, too quickly after deciding to start up their business. You should not spend hundreds of dollars on advertising in the beginning. Remember that your ideal number one advertisement will be word of mouth.

People you complete projects for that are happy with your services, will want to tell their friends. As for dissatisfied customers, according to a Minnesota firm that performs customer satisfaction surveys, studies show that most unsatisfied customers never talk to the company with whom they are dissatisfied, but they are far from quiet about their problems. Instead of talking to you, they will talk to your potential customers (their friends) and even your competitors!

Dissatisfied customers tell an average of ten other people about their bad experience. With these statistics, you want to provide superior customer service to ensure you satisfy your customer's needs completely! Other than word of mouth, there are ways to get your name out there, which will be discussed in much more detail in the marketing section of this book. But for now, do not spend a lot of money on advertising.

Spend more time learning everything you can about the different marketing techniques and possibilities, so you can select the least expensive and sometimes free methods to help keep your start-up costs low. You may find that you never need to place large newspaper ads, and can rely mostly upon referrals from your customers and the telephone book…or even better yet, have most of your customers come to you!

Dress Code

The appropriate clothing for your business depends on the area of specialization, the clients you will cater to the most, and the stage of the project. In the beginning, you should always meet with a prospective customer in appropriate business attire – business casual at the very least. If you are working with a professional office helping them organize files or storage areas, you should dress business professional. Match your attire to the business you are dealing with, and never "stick out like a sore thumb."

In general, there are two types of customers you will be working with: Residential and Business. There are also two stages to every project you complete: stage one is the initial contact and assessment phase, and stage two is the project completion phase. You want to keep the phase of the project in mind when choosing your attire.

Residential Organizing: If you are organizing for a residential customer, during phase two it is appropriate to dress casually. By causal, I mean, a pair of casual slacks or clean jeans, a casual shirt and casual shoes (I do not recommend sneakers unless you'll be moving a considerable amount of furniture or larger items.) When you are hired to complete a project for a residential customer, I recommend discussing your planned attire with your customers, and explain what they should wear as well, since they will be helping you in most situations. This way, you will not have to wait while the client changes into appropriate clothes when you are ready to dive into a project, and you will not embarrass them by showing up in casual slacks and a casual shirt when they have on "painting clothes."

Business Organizing: If you are organizing for a business, appropriate attire is at minimum – business casual. Keep a watchful eye during your initial visit(s) to see what employees around the office are wearing. You will be able to see if the office dress code is business casual or business professional. You want to "fit in," so you do not appear out of place when you are completing the project. Of course, if you'll be completing the project in an out-of-the way place, such as a storage closet or a place where you will get dirty, you may want to dress business casual. But if you will be working out in the open or in an area that has considerable traffic, your client will appreciate the extra effort and detail you take to dress appropriately for the environment. For further clarification, business casual would be a pair of khaki's or plain black slacks, or a conservative skirt, and a business blouse/shirt, or even a casual dress. Business professional is a business suit, dress suit and tie (for men).

Workshops: If you are coaching or consulting, business casual or business professional is the most appropriate attire. The rule of thumb is, you should always dress one step more professional than your audience.

Business Casual for Women

Business Casual for Men

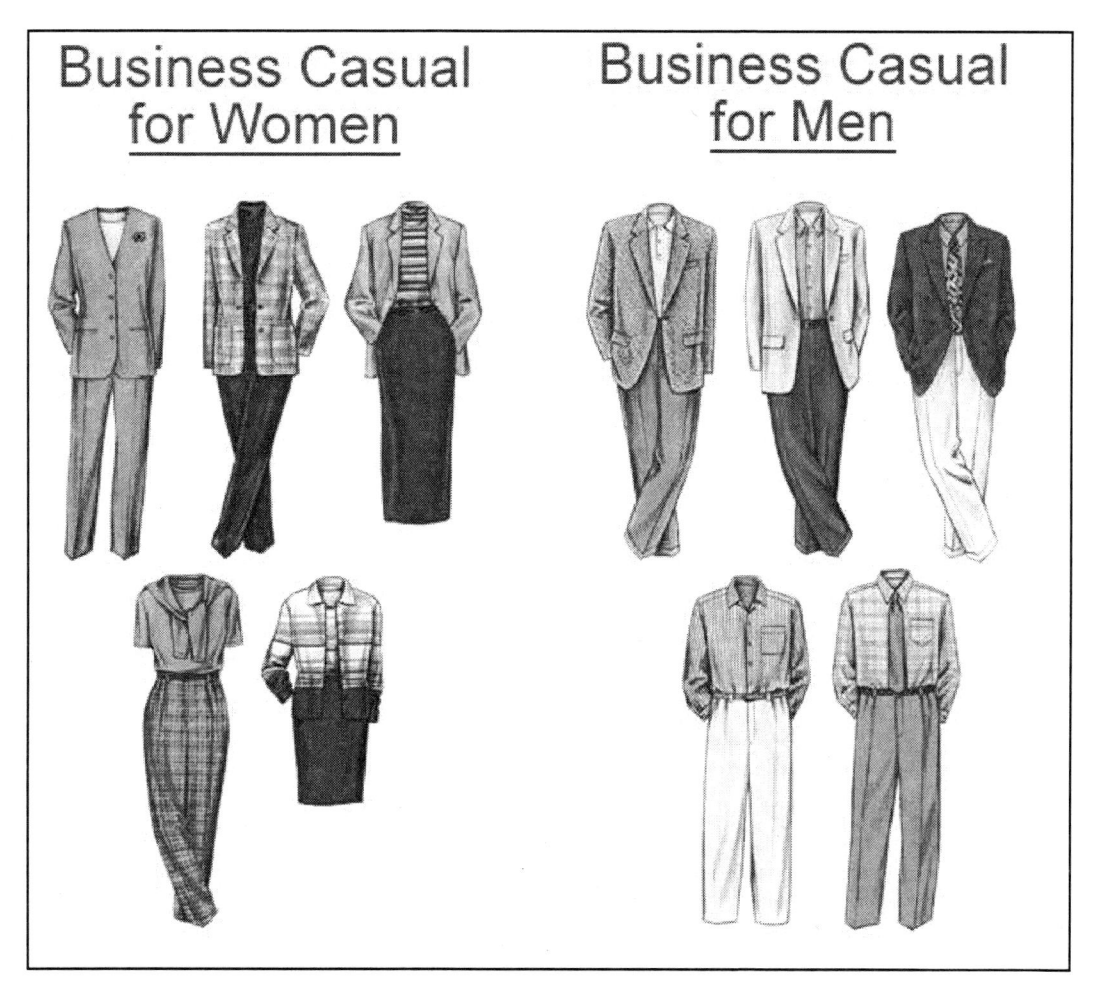

This picture gives you an idea of what businesses consider "business casual attire." With that in mind, business professional (a suit and tie or a business dress) is one step up from business casual (khaki's or light slacks). This gives you a guide to work from for determining your attire. Above all, arriving at the client's home or office in a pair of sweatpants and a T-shirt will diminish your integrity and professionalism.

Licensing Your Business

Once you determine you have a legitimate business (meaning you have paying customers), it is important for you to learn about licensing in your state/county/city. There are many different kinds of licenses, as well as many different forms of business you can classify your business as.

For this part, you will have to do a little research. If your business is located within an incorporated city, then the city will be your issuing agency. If your business is located outside of a city limit, then the county government will likely be your issuing agency. Fees for licenses vary, depending on the issuing agency and state. In general, they range from $25 to $300. Some government agencies have waiting periods to obtain licensing and others do not. Also, depending on your area of specialization, the state and local government agencies may require additional licenses. It is always best to contact your local city or county government agency first, and inquire about a business license.

Here is a list of the websites you can visit to obtain more information on state requirements for licensing your business. They are listed alphabetically by state (includes the District of Columbia): (Disclaimer: This list is accurate as of the publishing date of this book. Any errors or omissions are not the intent of the author and the author and publisher will not assume any liability or responsibility for the accuracy of this information.)

- Alabama - http://www.ador.state.al.us/licenses/authrity.html
- Alaska - http://www.dced.state.ak.us/occ/buslic.htm
- Arizona - http://www.revenue.state.az.us/license.htm
- Arkansas - http://www.state.ar.us/online_business.php
- California - http://www.calgold.ca.gov/
- Colorado - http://www.state.co.us/gov_dir/obd/blid.htm
- Connecticut - http://www.state.ct.us/
- Delaware - http://www.state.de.us/revenue/obt/obtmain.htm
- District of Columbia - http://www.dcra.dc.gov/
- Florida - http://sun6.dms.state.fl.us/dor/businesses/
- Georgia - http://www.sos.state.ga.us/corporations/regforms.htm
- Hawaii - http://www.hawaii.gov/dbedt/start/starting.html
- Idaho - http://www.idoc.state.id.us/Pages/BUSINESSPAGE.html
- Illinois - http://www.sos.state.il.us/departments/business_services/business.html
- Indiana - http://www.state.in.us/sic/owners/ia.html
- Iowa - http://www.iowasmart.com/blic/
- Kansas - http://www.accesskansas.org/operating/index.html
- Kentucky - http://www.thinkkentucky.com/kyedc/ebpermits.asp
- Louisiana - http://www.sec.state.la.us/comm/fss/fss-index.htm
- Maine - http://www.econdevmaine.com/biz-develop.htm
- Maryland - http://www.dllr.state.md.us/

- Massachusetts - http://www.state.ma.us/sec/cor/coridx.htm
- Michigan - http://medc.michigan.org/services/startups/index2.asp
- Minnesota - http://www.dted.state.mn.uss
- Mississippi - http://www.olemiss.edu/depts/mssbdc/going_intobus.html
- Missouri - http://www.ded.state.mo.us/business/businesscenter/
- Montana - http://www.state.mt.us/sos/biz.htm
- Nebraska - http://www.sos.state.ne.us/htm/businessmenu.htm
- New Hampshire - http://www.nhsbdc.org/startup.htm
- New Jersey - http://www.state.nj.us/njbiz/s_lic_and_cert.shtml
- New York - http://www.dos.state.ny.us/lcns/licensing.html
- New Mexico - http://www.state.nm.us/
- Nevada - http://dbi.state.nv.us/
- North Carolina - http://www.secstate.state.nc.us/secstate/blio/default.htm
- North Dakota - http://www.state.nd.us/sec/
- Ohio - http://www.state.oh.us/sos/business_services_information.htm
- Oklahoma - http://www.okonestop.com/
- Oregon - http://www.filinginoregon.com
- Pennsylvania - http://www.paopenforbusiness.state.pa.us
- Rhode Island - http://www.corps.state.ri.us/firststop/index.asp
- South Carolina - http://www.state.sd.us/STATE/sitecategory.cfm?mp=Licenses/Occupations
- South Dakota - http://www.sdgreatprofits.com/DBISD.htm
- Tennessee - http://www.state.tn.us/
- Texas - http://www.tded.state.tx.us/guide/
- Utah - http://www.commerce.state.ut.us/web/commerce/admin/licen.htm
- Vermont - http://www.sec.state.vt.us/

- Virginia - http://www.dba.state.va.us/licenses/

- Washington - http://www.wa.gov/dol/bpd/limsnet.htm

- West Virginia - http://www.state.wv.us/taxrev/busreg.html

- Wisconsin - http://www.wdfi.org/corporations/forms/

- Wyoming - http://soswy.state.wy.us/corporat/corporat.htm

Naming Your Business

For some people business names come easily, for others finding the right one is a major challenge. If you have difficulty coming up with a business name, you may need to examine ways to inspire your creativity to give you an initial list of names. Determining what name you choose is based upon your personal preferences. Some experienced entrepreneurs insist that a business name should be descriptive of the type of business you operate; others suggest being unique is the best way to be remembered.

Keep in mind that your business name is an important part of your marketing effort. It is a major component of how customers' perceive your business. Your business image is based on this perception. So, it is critical that the name you select reflects the image you want customers to have of your business.

I recommend you listen to what your inner voice says is right. You are the one who has to live with it business day and night for a long time to come. So choose something you feel good about. One test might be to think about the name being splashed across a major headline. How about, "(*business name*) Reports Phenomenal Profits"? How does it feel to see that name in print representing your business? If it feels good then go with it.

To find the right name for your business:

- Check for state regulations on naming a business. Many states require specific wording for corporations and LLC's. If your business will be structured as a sole proprietorship, you can name your business using an "alias" or "DBA: Doing Business As" assumption. For example, Jane Smith wants to name her business "Organization Simplified," and is opening it as a sole proprietorship. Her business alias would be "Organization Simplified" and her bank account would show: "Jane Smith, DBA Organization Simplified." (More details on business structure will be discussed in the next topic titled: Business Structure.)

- Make a list of names of similar businesses or those who are competitors.

- Decide how you would like to differentiate yourself from the other businesses.

- Consider how you want your business to be viewed by your customers.

- Make a list of possible names and test them on friends, family, and possible clients, asking not only whether they like the name, but also what the name conveys to them.

- Register or trademark your business name if desired, to protect others from using it.

Business Structure

There are a wide variety of ways to put together the operations of your business so it functions effectively and efficiently. The structure that works best for you will be related to your objectives, what your service specialty is, tax ramifications and your personal operational style. However, there are a number of functions that every business needs to address simply as part of doing business.

One of the first decisions that you will have to make as a business owner is how your company will be legally structured. The most popular legal structures for businesses are:

- Sole Proprietorship
- Partnership
- Corporation (a form of "incorporating" your business)
- Limited Liability Company (a form of "incorporating" your business)

This decision will have long-term implications, so you should consult with an accountant and attorney to help you select the form of ownership that is right for you. The following chart is designed to help you make your initial determination for the structure of your business: *(Disclaimer: You should consult an accountant and attorney to answer any questions you may have and help you determine and establish your business structure. The author accepts no liability for the information contained here.)*

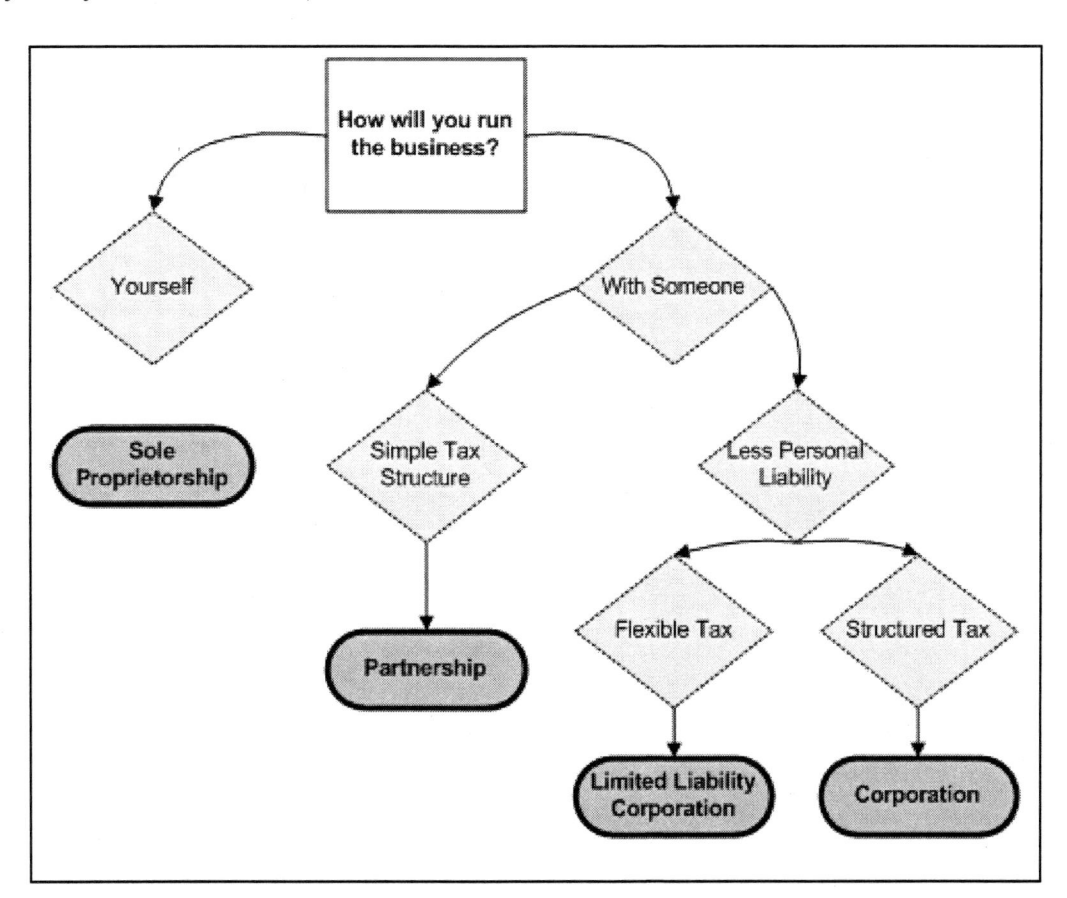

```
                    How will you run
                    the business?
                   /                \
              Yourself            With Someone
                 |               /            \
                 |         Simple Tax     Less Personal
                 |         Structure       Liability
                 |              |          /        \
              Sole              |     Flexible    Structured
          Proprietorship    Partnership   Tax        Tax
                                          |          |
                                   Limited Liability  Corporation
                                      Corporation
```

Sole Proprietorship: The vast majority of small businesses start out as sole proprietorships. One person owns a sole proprietorship business. It is usually the individual who has day-to-day responsibility for running the business. Sole proprietors own all the assets of the business and the profits generated by it. They also assume complete responsibility for all liabilities and/or debts. In the eyes of the law and the public, you – as owner, are one and the same with the business.

Advantages of a Sole Proprietorship

- Easiest and least expensive form of ownership to organize.
- Sole proprietors are in complete control, and within the parameters of the law, may make decisions as they see fit.
- Sole proprietors receive all income generated by the business to keep or reinvest.
- Profits from the business flow-through directly to the owner's personal tax return.
- The business is easy to dissolve, if desired.

Disadvantages of a Sole Proprietorship

- Sole proprietors have unlimited liability and are legally responsible for all debts against the business. Their business *and* personal assets are at risk.
- May be at a disadvantage in raising funds and are often limited to using funds from personal savings or consumer loans.
- May have a hard time attracting high-caliber employees, or those that are motivated by the opportunity to own a part of the business.
- Some employee benefits such as owner's medical insurance premiums are not **directly** deductible from business income (only partially deductible as an adjustment to income).

To Form a Sole Proprietorship:

1. Choose the type of business you wish to operate.
2. Pick a name for the business.
3. Register the name with the appropriate local or state office. (If you use a "DBA – Doing Business As" name, you do not need to register the name of your business.)
4. Obtain licensing to conduct the business (if needed).
5. Determine where the business will be located.

Federal Tax Forms for Sole Proprietorship *(only a partial list and some may not apply)*
- Form 1040: Individual Income Tax Return
- Schedule C: Profit or Loss from Business (or Schedule C-EZ)
- Schedule SE: Self-Employment Tax
- Form 1040-ES: Estimated Tax for Individuals
- Form 4562: Depreciation and Amortization
- Form 8829: Expenses for Business Use of your Home
- Employment Tax Forms

Partnership: A partnership is a business entity in which two or more individuals carry on a continuing business for profit as co-owners. Legally, a partnership is regarded as a group of individuals rather than as a single entity, although each of the partners files their share of the profits on their individual tax returns. A business partnership is an agreement between two or more individuals to operate a business jointly. Partners are responsible for the other partner's business actions, as well as their own.

To Form a Partnership:
1. List the amount of equity to be invested by each partner.
2. Determine how the profit or loss will be divided among the partners.
3. Establish compensation levels for each partner, including when the compensation will be given and any restrictions that might affect that compensation.
4. Set guidelines for how the business will be modified or dissolved should one or more partners wish to end the partnership.
5. Define procedures for settling any disputes that might arise.
6. Determine who has authority for which expenditures and how expenditure decisions are to be made.
7. Develop procedures to follow in case of death or incapacitation of a partner.
8. Write and sign an agreement detailing the responses to the questions above.
9. A general partnership can be formed simply by an oral agreement, but a legal partnership agreement drawn up by an attorney is highly recommended. (A sample *Partnership Agreement* can be found in Appendix A, Form 51.)

Corporation: A corporation, chartered by the state in which it is headquartered, is considered by law to be a unique entity, separate and apart from those who own it. A corporation can be taxed; it can be sued; it can enter into contractual agreements. The owners of a corporation are its shareholders. The shareholders elect a board of directors to oversee the major policies and decisions. The corporation has a life of its own and does not dissolve when ownership changes. There are four characteristics that define corporations: 1.) Limited liability to the extent of assets, 2.) Continuity of life, 3.) Centralization of management, 4.) Free transferability of ownership interests.

Advantages of a Corporation

- Shareholders have limited liability for the corporation's debts or judgments against the corporations.

- Generally, shareholders can only be held accountable for their investment in stock of the company. (Note however, that officers can be held personally liable for their actions, such as the failure to withhold and pay employment taxes.)

- Corporations can raise additional funds through the sale of stock.

- A corporation may deduct the cost of benefits it provides to officers and employees.

- Can elect S corporation status if certain requirements are met. This election enables company to be taxed similar to a partnership.

Disadvantages of a Corporation

- The process of incorporation requires more time and money than other forms of organization.

- Corporations are monitored by federal, state and some local agencies, and as a result may have more paperwork to comply with regulations.

- Incorporating may result in higher overall taxes. Dividends paid to shareholders are not deductible from business income, thus this income can be taxed twice.

To Form a Corporation:

1. Pick a name for the corporation.

2. Prepare and file *Articles of Incorporation* (Appendix A, Form 8).

3. Choose a Board of Directors.

4. Adopt bylaws.

5. Develop the financing plans for the corporation.

6. Establish a Corporate Bank Account.

7. Set up a record keeping system.

8. Hold a Directors' Meeting.

9. Decide whether to file S Corporation Election (owners reports their share of corporate profits on their personal tax returns).

Federal Tax Forms for Regular or "C" Corporations *(only a partial list and some may not apply)*
- Form 1120 or 1120-A: Corporation Income Tax Return
- Form 1120-W: Estimated Tax for Corporation
- Form 8109-B: Deposit Coupon
- Form 4625: Depreciation
- Employment Tax Forms
- Other forms as needed for capital gains, sale of assets, alternative minimum tax, etc.

Limited Liability Company (LLC): The LLC is a relatively new type of hybrid business structure that is now permissible in most states. It is designed to provide the limited liability features of a corporation and the tax efficiencies and operational flexibility of a partnership. Formation is more complex and formal than that of a general partnership. The owners are members, and the duration of the LLC is usually determined when the organization papers are filed. The time limit can be continued if desired by a vote of the members at the time of expiration. LLC's must not have more than two of the four characteristics that define corporations: 1.) Limited liability to the extent of assets, 2.) Continuity of life, 3.) Centralization of management, 4.) Free transferability of ownership interests.

To form a Limited Liability Company (LLC):

1. Choose a name which complies with your state law for LLC's.

2. Prepare and file Articles of Organization with your state LLC office.

3. Draw up the Operating Agreement among the owners.

4. Set up a bank account for the LLC.

Federal Tax Forms for LLC

An LLC is taxed as a partnership in most cases; corporation forms must be used if there are more than two of the four corporate characteristics, as described above.

Federal Employer Identification Number (EIN)

What It Is: An Employer Identification Number (EIN), also known as a Federal Tax Identification Number, is a nine-digit number that the IRS assigns to business entities. The IRS uses this number to identify taxpayers that are required to file various business tax returns. Employers, sole proprietors, corporations, partnerships, non-profit organizations, trusts and estates, government agencies, certain individuals and other business entities use EINs.

Who Needs It: Regardless of your type of business, if you have employees, you are required to obtain an EIN, which you can now apply for either by mail, fax, telephone or online. In most cases, you can obtain your EIN number immediately so you can open your business banking accounts and obtain the necessary licenses, and the government will mail a confirmation to you. If you are self-employed as a sole proprietor, you are not required to obtain an EIN. You can use your social security number as your tax identification number, even for opening a banking account.

How To Apply: There are four methods for applying for a Federal EIN. They are:

1. Online
2. Tele-TIN
3. Fax-TIN
4. Mail SS-4 Application

Online Application: You may file online for your EIN. The online address is: https://sa1.www4.irs.gov/sa_vign/newFormSS4.do. The process is relatively easy, and there are online help menu's to assist you if you have difficulty completing the online application process. Once you complete and submit the online application, you will be provided with what the IRS calls a "provisional EIN." This will be your permanent EIN unless there is a problem with processing, so you may use the EIN immediately to open bank accounts and apply for a business license (if needed).

> **Who may not apply online:** The online application process is not available as of the publishing of this book for the following types of entities: Foreign Addresses (including Puerto Rico), Limited Liability Company (LLC) without entity types, State and Local Governments, Federal Government, Military, and Indian Tribal Government or Enterprise. You should call the toll-free Business and Specialty Tax Line at 1-800-829-4933, if you need assistance applying for an EIN. Foreign Addresses (addresses outside the continental USA, Alaska and Hawaii) should call (215) 516-6999.

Tele-TIN: You may also call the Internal Revenue Service and provide them with your company information over the telephone to apply for your EIN. This process is very easy, and can usually be completed in ten minutes or less. The telephone number you call is determined by the state your business is located in, and can be found on the chart provided on page 23 under "EIN Address and Phone Information."

Fax-TIN: You may fax the *SS-4 – Application for EIN* (located on the Forms CD, Form 60) for your convenience or downloadable at: http://www.irs.gov/pub/irs-pdf/fss4.pdf). Once you complete the application, fax it to the number listed based on the state your business is located in, provided on page 23 under "EIN Address and Phone Information."

Mail: You may mail the *SS-4 – Application for EIN* (Forms CD, Form 60 or downloadable at: http://www.irs.gov/pub/irs-pdf/ffs4.pdf). Once you complete the application, mail it to the address based on the state your business is located in, provided in the chart at the bottom of this page.

Keep A Record of Your Application: Be sure to keep a paper copy of the SS-4 or online application for your records.

EIN Address and Phone Information*

If your principal business, office or agency, or legal residence (in the case of an individual), is located in:	Call the Tele-TIN or Fax-TIN number shown or mail to the "Internal Revenue Service Center" at:
Connecticut, Delaware, District of Columbia, Florida, Georgia, Maine, Maryland, Massachusetts, New Hampshire, New Jersey, New York, North Carolina, Ohio, Pennsylvania, Rhode Island, South Carolina, Vermont, Virginia, West Virginia	Attn: EIN Operation Holtsville, NY 00501 Business and Specialty Tax Line (Obtain an EIN from 7:30am -5:30pm local time only): (800) 829-4933 Fax-TIN: (631) 447-8960
Illinois, Indiana, Kentucky, Michigan	Attn: EIN Operation Cincinnati, OH 45999 Business and Specialty Tax Line (Obtain an EIN from 7:30am -5:30pm local time only): (800) 829-4933 Fax-TIN: (859) 669-5760
Alabama, Alaska, Arizona, Arkansas, California, Colorado, Hawaii, Idaho, Iowa, Kansas, Louisiana, Minnesota, Mississippi, Missouri, Montana, Nebraska, Nevada, New Mexico, North Dakota, Oklahoma, Oregon, Puerto Rico, South Dakota, Tennessee, Texas, Utah, Washington, Wisconsin, Wyoming	Attn: EIN Operation Philadelphia, PA 19255 Business and Specialty Tax Line (Obtain an EIN from 7:30am -5:30pm local time only): (800) 829-4933 Fax-TIN: (215) 516-3990
If you have no legal residence, principal place of business, or principal office or agency in any state:	Attn: EIN Operation Philadelphia, PA 19255 Business and Specialty Tax Line (Obtain an EIN from 7:30am -5:30pm local time only): (800) 829-4933 Fax-TIN: (215) 516-3990

*Taken from http://www.irs.gov/businesses/small/article/0,,id=97851,00.html.

Financial Institutions and Bank Accounts

How should you choose a bank or financial institution? Unfortunately most business owners do not thoroughly consider their needs when selecting a financial institution. Although there are laws and regulations that govern the activities of banks, savings and loans and credit unions, not all financial institutions are the same. Each institution establishes its own policies for:

- Types of products and services that are offered
- Criteria for loan qualification
- Minimum balances for accounts
- Interest rates
- Charges for account services

While one bank may specialize in home or auto loans, another may focus on commercial loans for businesses. Some banks may only offer basic deposit accounts, while others have safe deposit boxes, sweep accounts, and even online banking. It is very important that you evaluate your business needs before you select your bank. Consider some of the things your banker will help you with. They can:

- Assist you with the cash management needs of your business.
- Offer investment products of varying maturities and risks.
- Offer loans appropriate to meet your needs.

So compare financial institutions in order to find the one that will serve your business's needs and will also provide the high support and assistance you need during all the stages of your business, beginning with infancy. Selecting an institution that you can work with will be especially important as your business grows. Some tips to assist you in making a good decision are:

- Approach the decision as a long-term investment.
- Ask your accountant or lawyer to introduce you to bankers that they are familiar with. Go to your regular bank, and speak with someone you know there about business services.
- Check with your local chamber of commerce to find out what banks are active in the community. Attend their meetings or other service organizations to meet bankers that are involved and have interests similar to your own.
- Look for a complementary personality, someone you can relate to.
- Introduce yourself to the banking center manager.
- Find out how long they have been in their current position (note that many bank managers and officers change locations and get promoted).
- Tell them about your business and the form of organization you are starting, so they can tell you what special products and services or restrictions might apply.

At a time when there appears to be a different bank going up on every corner, and all of them competing for your attention, it is important for you to choose the right financial institution and the right account for the cash management of your business.

There are a few banks in the country (as of the writing of this book) that offer "free small business checking," and they usually charge no fees as long as you remain under a certain number of transactions per statement period (usually a month). Some banks have special fee-free accounts, provided you meet a specific combined balance between all of your business and personal accounts that are held at the same institution.

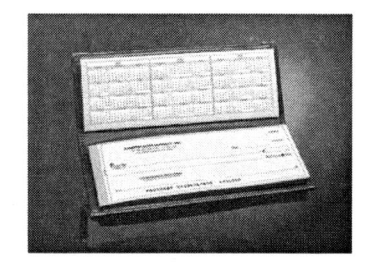

Regardless of the type of account you select, I recommend you it simple in the beginning. It is not necessary for the success of your business to spend considerable money when you order checks. You can spend a great deal of money on legal size checks, or 3-ring binder check keeping systems. Some bankers may lead you to believe you are required to have business size checks for business accounts, which is not true. The most important components on a check is the routing number, the account number, and your business name and address; not the size or style of check. Keep your costs as low as you can. Some banks permit you to order checks through a third party check printer, and you can usually find standard size checks at a considerable savings. Some websites of third party check printers are:

- http://www.checksunlimited.com
- http://www.checkworks.com
- http://www.compuchecks.com
- http://www.designerchecks.com

If you order personal size checks from a third party company, they usually include deposit slips at the back of each book of checks. If you need more, you can order a box of personal or business size deposit slips from the mail order check printer.

Once you have your business bank account established, use it to transact all your business finances. Pay all bills and make all purchases through that account, and deposit all income into the account. If you need to "pay yourself," then write yourself a check from the business account and deposit it into your personal account for tracking purposes. Always try to transact your business so you have an audit trail. Keep receipts for everything, and above all else, keep your business finances separate from your personal finances.

External Funding and Loans

The start-up costs of this type of business are relatively low (provided you do not go "overboard" on your initial purchases and expenses), so the need for private investors, or even loans from banks or finance companies is normally not necessary. If you are a good organizer, it means you are probably very industrious, and you can try to get by without additional financing.

If you have no resources at all, you may need to consider alternatives to fund the costs of starting your business. Finding the right financing that fits with a business' goals is a continuing challenge for almost every small business. For start-up businesses this can be one of the biggest hurdles in getting off the ground.

Some business owners can be very creative in finding ways to fund their ventures. As mentioned earlier in this book, many people work another job as a way to fund their personal business. Most companies, however, find their start-up funding in more conventional ways. According to Judith Kautz, author of the website www.smallbusinessnotes.com, the most common sources are:

- 72% Personal Savings
- 45% Banks
- 28% Friends/Relatives
- 10% Individual Investors
- 7% Government-guaranteed Loans
- 1% Venture Capital Firms

Using personal funds is very common, partly because few banks will loan to people who do not risk some of their personal funds. The old-fashioned wisdom in starting a business is that no financial institution or lender will loan money to a start-up business. With no business history and not enough assets, a small business owner either needs to have savings, or friends and family who are willing to help. While there are many challenges to obtaining financing or funding, loans do exist, and with reasonable preparation, they may even be relatively easy to obtain.

The first step in seeking external funding is to be prepared. As discussed earlier, you do not normally need to write a business plan for a small business of this type, but if you are seeking external funding, you will need one. You will also need to prepare financial statements, line up references, develop a clear definition of what the business enterprise is, and look at how you rate on other factors such as your credit rating, financial history, and business planning that lenders consider in awarding loans.

Learn the lending language. Do your research online for small business lending. It can be embarrassing to misuse terms. That immediately labels you as someone who has not done his or her homework - and consequently is not a good investment candidate.

Find out which are the right banks to approach if you want to go that route. The Small Business Administration has a list of commercial banks, which scores them on how aggressive they are in small business lending. The website is: http://www.sba.gov/gopher/Local-Information/Certified-Preferred-Lenders/.

One of the toughest questions to answer is how much capital is enough. A quick model for cash needs suggests determining how much capital is needed for one year of operation. That first year, keep your initial capital separate from your income. That income should then be the initial capital for the second year. Amounts you will need to finance are the initial capital and any growth you want to introduce above and beyond the initial model. Many companies that are successful today have started that simply.

Chapter 3

3: Money Matters

What Income You Can Expect

How much money you make is entirely up to you! How successful do you plan on being? How hard are you willing to work for it? Are you willing to endure the ups and the downs, and set goals based on your knowledge, your skills, your creativity and your dedication? That's the glory of having a business of your own. You can set your own goals, and reach them, even far exceed your own expectations, as you watch your business bloom into a lucrative endeavor.

Regardless of your specialty in the organizing business, you may decide to complete one to four projects a month, and make from $100 to $1800 per month. If you set some defining goals for yourself, and work a bit harder, or decide to expand and do seminars, create newsletters, write a book, create a product, or even hire employees while you "manage" the business, you can literally make thousands of dollars per month. So the real questions you should be asking yourself are…how much work do you want to put into it, and how much money do you want to make?

Quoting Your Project

There are three plans for pricing your project: hourly rate plan, per-project rate plan, and small, medium and large rate plan. Regardless of your method of pricing, once you quote a project, you should always honor your original price. If you do not honor your original quote, you will lose repeat customers and risk burning bridges. Remember that errors happen.

If you quote a project too high, you can offer your customer a percentage discount, even if you have already begun the project. You might ask them if they would be willing to allow you to list them as a referral for future business, or write a testimonial for a discount. Most customers will be delighted to do this for you, and you will feel better that you have not over charged your customer.

Hourly Rate

If you are new to the organizing business, the easiest way to determine a project cost is to charge a per hour rate. An appropriate hourly rate ranges from $30 to $60 per hour. You should not tell your customer that you charge an hourly rate, because you may not be given the opportunity to provide the service. Instead, estimate the time it will take you to complete the job and multiply it by your hourly rate and you have your price quote. For example, if you determine a project will take 10 hours to complete and you charge $45 per hour, your proposal would show the project cost at $450 (10 x $45 = $450).

Per Project Rate

Once you have been in business for a while, you may want to establish per project rates rather than using an hourly rate. If you know it usually takes the same amount of time to organize a specific area, you may establish a flat fee. For example, if you know from experience that it takes 8 hours to organize a four-drawer filing cabinet, and you charge $45 per hour, you can establish a flat fee of $360 for organizing all 4-drawer filing cabinets (8 x $45 = $360).

Regardless of which method you use to quote a price for your customer, remember that experience and knowledge is the key to getting it right. You will know in time if your fee is too high or too low. A successful businessperson evaluates the finances regularly and makes any necessary changes.

Small, Medium, and Large Rate Plan

You may prefer a rate plan based on the average total amount of time it takes to complete a project, and establish a flat fee for that time frame. For example:

Small Project	**Medium Project**	**Large Project**
Up to 8 hours	9-16 hours	17-24 hours
$400	$800	$1200

Estimating Project Completion Time

Since your business largely relies upon the time it takes to complete a project, you need to develop a firm understanding of the length of time it takes to complete certain tasks. Estimating time of completion is one area that is tough to define because there are many variables. Some factors you should take into consideration during your assessment are: the location of the project, the number of people assisting, your client's willingness to help, and any obstacles you may encounter. (The assessment is more thoroughly explained in Chapter 6.)

This is an area where doing free jobs or "sample" jobs in your own house will help you. Completely empty out your closet, and organize it just like you would for a customer. How long did it take you? What obstacles did you encounter and what did it take to overcome them? What did or didn't you anticipate? Did you have help? Were you dealing with a large or small quantity of items?

Do the same sample job for your friends and relatives. Take Grandma's file cabinet and organize it free of charge. Note the time it takes, Grandma's willingness to throw things out, her level of help, and obstacles you encountered.

Once you have general information from your sample jobs, you can use that information to estimate future jobs. Keep in mind that for nearly all projects, your customer should help you. Another thing to consider is you should avoid completing large projects in one session. If you have eight hours of work to complete, you should break it up into two sessions of four hours each. There are instances when a customer prefers a project be completed in one session. If so, it is appropriate to ask your customer to employ the help of friends. Remember that the customer is paying for your expertise, not your physical labor.

It is appropriate to discuss interruptions with your customers in advance. If they have children, an arrangement should be made so you can work on the project without distraction. Every little distraction takes time away from the completion of your project.

Products Required For Project

Regardless of the project you are completing, you will need some products and/or supplies that the customer will keep. The general rule of thumb is if the customer keeps it, the customer pays for it. There are four methods used to purchase supplies. They are:

- Organizer's Supply Catalog
- Allowance
- Supply Price List
- Customer's Supply Catalog

The most preferred method for ordering supplies that the customer will keep is to utilize an Organizer's Supply Catalog. Many office supply and organization supply companies produce catalogs that you can order free of charge. You should take your catalogs with you during the assessment, and upon determining the supplies you need, allow the customer to select the specific items from your catalogs. Once the customer makes a decision, they call the companies and place the orders themselves, using their own preferred method of payment, and arranging for the items to be shipped to their address prior to the start of the project. This method is the easiest and most preferred because the customer has the convenience of picking out the exact color, style, and type of items they want. No physical money or checks need to exchange hands between you and the customer, because the items are ordered directly through the supplier.

The second method is to have the customer establish an "allowance." This is a budgeted amount the organizer is allowed to spend on supplies. The organizer purchases the supplies (with or without the assistance/presence of the customer) and delivers the items to the customer at the start of the project.

This method requires making arrangements with the customer to pay you the allowed amount up front (and you return any unused portion) or reimburse you after you purchase and deliver the supplies (remember to keep the receipts for proof of your spending).

The third method is to establish a Supply Price List of standard items that you always have on hand, such as file folders, labels, dividers, trays, baskets, etc. More experienced organizers use a combination of this method and the Organizer's Supply Catalog method. File folders, labels, trays, etc., are items that you will use for most standard projects. Many organizers establish a "per item" fee, and charge the customer based on the number of items used. This is easier than other methods for **commonly** used supplies, because you may not know in advance exactly how many items you will need, and having them on hand makes it easier to utilize them as you work on the project.

The fourth and final method for obtaining supplies, the Customer's Supply Catalog, is the least preferred. Some organizers create their own catalog of supplies. Any items that are used for the project completion are purchased directly from, and delivered by the organizer. This method allows organizers to use the same "standard" items for all their projects, and to purchase those items through a discount supplier. The organizer then adds an up-charge to each item, and collects a small profit from the sales.

The reason I do not recommend this method is in two parts. One, the customer does not have as many options on color, type, style, etc. Since the customer must live with the supplies and use them after you are finished with the project, I believe in using items they prefer, and not items you prefer. Second, there is considerable work involved in creating your own catalog(s), and many organizers need to keep an inventory of standard items. This raises your start-up and business maintenance costs, as well as your accounting efforts, due to having inventory to track.

Regardless of the method you select, you should not add the cost of supplies to your rate plan for the project. It should be listed on a separate line on the quote or invoice. Make sure you indicate that the cost of supplies is a charge your customer will be responsible for paying in addition to your rate plan.

Below is a list of some popular supply company websites, where you can request free catalogs and order supplies:

- Office Depot: www.officedepot.com
- Office Max: www.officemax.com
- Staples: www.staples.com
- Viking Office Products: www.vikingop.com
- Corporate Express: www.corporateexpress.com
- Easy Closets: www.easyclosets.com
- File Wise: www.filewise.com
- Organize Everything: www.organize-everything.com

Deposit Requests

Once your customer agrees to an organizing project, it is reasonable for you to ask for a deposit. They are, after all, reserving your time to complete the project, and it ensures they are serious about paying for your services. It is reasonable to waive a deposit for a repeat client, or for a very small project.

A reasonable deposit amount is 10 - 20% of the project quote. Some professional organizers charge a flat fee for a deposit, such as $100, especially if the project will be a large and expensive one. It is also convenient to charge a flat deposit fee because there are no last minute calculations to worry about.

Remember that if you charge your customer a deposit, you need to subtract the deposit amount from the invoice total. You should always have a cancellation agreement to protect yourself, in case your customers change their minds about the project prior to the date it is expected to begin. Establish your policy in advance, put it in writing, and obtain your customer's signature prior to accepting the deposit, so there are no surprises. I also advise that if the customer pays you by personal check, you should exchange it for a cashier's check at their bank, or deposit it into your account and ensure it clears prior to the project start date.

The Nickel and Dime Syndrome

Webster's dictionary defines the phrase "Nickel and Dime" as: "Being charged for every little thing. Each charge is tolerable, but in concert, significant."

Charging a customer for every little thing you can think of is not only insignificant, it is unprofessional. The Nickel and Dime Syndrome can create a considerable strain on your business relationship with your customer. You should not charge for things such as: fuel costs, meals, mileage, driving time, paper for invoices, and "made up charges" such as tape measure usage fees, ink usage fees, etc.

If a project is located 20 or more miles outside of your local area, it is reasonable to charge mileage, provided your customer agrees to the expense in advance. Keep in mind that if you establish a "per-mile" fee, you should not double charge your customer by expecting fuel reimbursement as well. Use one method or the other.

Settling The Final Bill

Accepting Credit Cards: Once your business is established, you may want to talk to your bank about setting up a merchant account, so you can accept credit cards for payment. There are fees involved in credit card processing, which vary depending on the merchant you select to handle your transactions. There are many Internet merchant account companies that are less than honest, so be careful about the company you select. Most banks have a reputable company they deal with, and they can refer you or help you get the process started.

Collecting Final Payment: A large mistake many new organizers make is to leave the customer's home or office without collecting the final payment. Billing your customer after you leave opens up a whole new area of problems, and inevitably results in having your bill paid late, or not at all.

If you complete a small project, you should request the entire balance in full at the completion of the project. If you have a large project that occurs in multiple sessions, you may request payments in regularly scheduled intervals at the end of each session.

Receipts: Whenever the customer makes a payment, you should always write them a receipt. There is a template for *Receipts* in Appendix A, Form 57, or you can purchase an inexpensive pad of receipts from an office supply store.

Bad Checks: If for some reason, the customer's check is returned due to insufficient funds or a closed account after the project is completed, you will have to take some steps to collect it. It is reasonable for you to charge the customer fees to recover your costs (bank fees to your account for returned items, notices, phone calls, etc.). The first step to take would be to call the customer and inform them that their bank has returned the check unpaid. Avoid embarrassing your customer, as it may have been an oversight or honest mistake. Ask them for full payment within one week by money order or cashier's check. If you do not receive payment within the agreed time frame, follow the steps outlined in the next paragraph.

Correspondence For Nonpayment: If you do not get paid within one week, you should begin sending correspondence to the customer, with each letter being slightly stronger than the previous. Send your letters via certified mail with return receipt, so you have proof of notification if you need it, in the event that you have to take legal action. I have included three customizable collection letters in this book. They are *Collection Letter – NSF Check* (Appendix A, Form 25), *Collection Letter – Overdue Account* (Appendix A, Form 26) and *Collection Letter – Second Reminder* (Appendix A, Form 27).

Legal Action: If you are unable to collect after one phone call and three letters, you should seek the advice of legal counsel to determine if you should pursue the matter further. You may also want to consider small claims court if the amount owed is less than $5000 (depending on your state of residence). More information regarding filing legal action can be obtained from your local small claims court clerk.

Chapter 4

4: Marketing 101

Your Marketing Approach

When it comes to marketing your business, taking a laid-back approach is not the answer to success. You need to do more than just run some advertisements and announce your business, then sit back and wait for the telephone to ring. In the banking business, one thing I always tried to get my employees to understand is that no matter what the circumstances, you are always going to lose some customers. Some customers get job transfers and move, some get discouraged because of poor service, some are enticed by a better deal elsewhere, and some customers simply do not need your services anymore.

It is very important to your success to realize that the marketing of your business – generating new customers – is probably more important than the actual organizing services that you perform. I have listened to countless tellers at the bank say, "I'm a teller, not a seller." My response was – "The best teller is one who keeps a keen eye on what is best for their customers, and if you know a particular service will benefit your dedicated customers, why wouldn't you want to let them know about it?" You simply must generate new business to remain successful, even when you have repeat customers.

You need to understand now, before you go any further, that marketing is the key to getting and keeping your customers.

Create A Marketing Plan

The first step to becoming a marketing genius is to create a marketing plan. There is a distinct difference between a "marketing plan" and a "business plan."

A business plan is a complete description of your business, beginning with the basics. It projects your anticipated sales, expenses and profit over an extended period of time. A business plan is mostly needed if you are going to try to obtain a business loan or attract investors.

A marketing plan, on the other hand, is a plan you write that describes who your target audience is, details your product(s) and service(s), and indicates how you plan to generate prospects, and turn them into customers.

Unless you plan on getting a business loan or having private investors, I do not recommend wasting your time and effort on creating a business plan.

What you want to spend time on is devising a marketing plan. You already know some of the information for your marketing plan, such as what you want to sell (organizing services). Basically, you need to answer the following questions in writing, and revise it as time goes by so you can stay ahead of any changes that occur in your business.

- What product or service do you plan to sell?
- Who will you perform this service for?
- How will you generate (attract) prospects?
- How will you convert your prospects into customers?

A Reality Check

Now it is time for a reality check. If you are ambitious and set distinctive goals to accomplish in establishing and building your professional organizing business, you can expect to spend 50% or more of your time on marketing. Your marketing strategy takes time to plan, implement and even improve upon. You will constantly have to stay on top of your marketing plan and evaluate your success, and make changes if necessary. It is not something you can just put into action once, and then walk away from, while it works on its own. It takes time and effort. You must be willing to do the work to get the results you want.

Your Marketing Strategy

Just as you need a recipe to make cookies or cakes, you need a recipe to market. This is otherwise known as a "marketing strategy." Creating your marketing strategy does not have to be complicated. Begin by asking yourself some questions:

- Who do you want to perform your services for?
- Are there enough customers who need your services?
- How will you generate prospects?
- What specific services or products do your prospects want?
- Answer your prospects question: "What can you do for me?" (It has to be helpful to the prospect and profitable enough for you to do.)
- How will you convert your prospects into customers?
- What repeat services can you offer to your customers?
- How do you let existing customers know you have other services to offer?

You may not be able to answer all these questions right away. As a matter of fact, you should not be able to answer them all immediately. It takes time to make a business grow and prosper. It is not like deciding you are going to buy a new purse, then running to the nearest department store, and walking out with it a few minutes later.

Cold Calls, Prospects and Customers

On the CD, I have included a Microsoft Access database named *Database - Contact Management* (instructions for using located in Appendix B, database located on companion *Forms CD*). If you have a computer and Microsoft Office 2000 or later, you should have no problem using the database. If you prefer, I have included a Microsoft Excel spreadsheet named *Customer Management List* (Appendix A, Form 28). In the event that you do not have a computer, I recommend you invest in an index card file and some blank index cards, or a good size address book to keep track of your contacts. I have also included a sheet named *Prospect Data Sheet* (Appendix A, Form 55) that you can keep track of by hand if you prefer.

There are three basic kinds of contacts.

Cold Calls: Cold calls are people you do not know yet. They have not contacted you, nor have you spoken with or met them. They are unknown potential customers. Some examples of cold calls might be a list of names from the phone book, unknown subscribers to a religious or trade newspaper that you advertise in, or even a list of names you purchased from a marketing research group. Your prospects will often come from your cold calls.

Prospects: Prospects are people who you have spoken with or been in some form of contact with. They usually come from your cold calls, and they contact you about your services or a particular offer you advertise. Once a person contacts you, you should immediately change their status in your database from cold call to prospect, or add them if you have not done so previously.

Customers: These are people who have purchased your services or products. If they have given you money for a service or product, then they are a customer, and should be listed in your customer database. They are very important because they may have a need for additional services and may even send you referrals.

When a contact is a cold call, and they call you for information, they become a prospect. So it is appropriate for you to mark that person as a prospect. If you are able to convert them into a customer, then you should mark them as a customer.

The *Database – Contact Management* (located on the companion *Forms CD*), *Customer Management List* (Appendix A, Form 28) and *Prospect Data Sheet* (Appendix A, Form 55) will help you keep close tabs on your contacts.

Planting The Seed For Future Business

I can climb upon my soapbox and write about "planting the seed" forever. As a former bank manager, I frequently encouraged the staff to look for opportunities to sell additional services to customers. One employee in particular became discouraged when a customer refused her recommendation for a free service. Many times, I explained to the employee that she was "planting the seed for future business," and that a customer is rarely sold on a service or product after the first recommendation.

How many times have you stood in the store staring at the same sweater, knowing you want it, but you hesitate anyway? The same holds true for your prospects. They know they want your services, but are not sure they need or can afford your services.

All these scenarios prove one thing: You cannot put an advertisement in the newspaper and expect to generate all your business from that one ad. In a perfect world, it would work, but at a time when consumers are being bombarded with advertisements, it is difficult to convince people to buy your services on the first try.

That is why you should have a prospect list. Prospects are the people who are "thinking about it." Your strategy should be to run ads, send letters, put signs and business cards on bulletin boards, submit press releases, run mailings with direct marketers, etc. to generate prospects.

Once you acquire prospects, you can be confident that they have genuine interest in your services. You should follow up with your prospects from time to time, which may help you convert some of them into customers.

Keep in mind that every disorganized person on earth will not be a prospect. Believe it or not, some people actually like their messes, and they will never move from a prospect to a customer. As my mother always says, it is "*MY* organized mess" and as difficult as it is for me to relate, I realize that she knows exactly where everything is, "and if you so much as touch it, you are in big trouble!"

Chapter 5

5: Marketing 201

Your Target Audience

How do you inform the public that you have valuable services that will benefit them? Choosing the right target audience for your marketing effort is the key to having the best response. For example, you will not want to put an advertisement in a marketing mailer sent to homeowners that highlights your "warehouse organizing" abilities. If you want to help homeowners, then you need to specifically target homeowners. The same holds true on the opposite end of the board. If you want to generate some business customers, you should not send them a mailer highlighting your "closet organizing" services. Put some thought into whom your audience is, and the services you want to sell.

However, do not allow what I just mentioned to discourage you from targeting multiple audiences. Try to focus on one target audience for each individual marketing effort, so you can provide the best offer to all of your prospects.

Your Offer

The first step to generating prospects is to create a compelling offer that will make your target audience respond. You should make this offer so interesting and inviting, that your audience simply cannot pass it up. You know the services you provide are excellent, which is a reason in itself to get your audience to stand up and take notice. In the same respect, know that people are very good at procrastinating by making excuses. Remember the sweater scenario in the last chapter…you know it is the perfect complement to your wardrobe, but for some reason, you contemplate the purchase anyway? The same goes for your target audience. There are many different reasons why your target audience contemplates the need for your services as well. Perhaps they believe they do not need a professional to motivate and organize their space. Perhaps they think your fees are too high, or they are too embarrassed to let you see their clutter. (Have you ever known someone who cleans their house before the cleaning people get there?) People tend to make many excuses for procrastinating, especially a project like organizing, sorting, cleaning and clutter control.

So you see, simply offering customers your services is not enough. Many first-time organizers think that offering a "free consultation" is the way to go. Think of what you would do if you were the prospect? Would you invite someone into your home for a "free consultation" if you were not sure you needed their services?

My husband finds it funny when I get Home Interior, Pampered Chef, or Secret Candles party invitations because I do not like getting them, since I know two things. One, I am inevitably going to buy something I do not want. I am going to a party, hosted by my friend, who ultimately wants some free stuff for having the party. I know that the more orders she gets, the more free stuff she can have. So out of obligation, I find one item that is reasonably priced. The second thing I know is that the hostess and sales person will be asking me if I want to have a party in my home, and if that word "obligation" is really a weak point for me, I will probably schedule one I do not want to have…which is most likely how my friend ended up having her party in the first place.

Do you see where I am going here? We do not want to say, "I am not a salesperson, but I really want to come into your home and give you my sales presentation." If we said this, how many people do you think would let us in? Of course, you will have a certain number of people who desperately need your services, and they may bite right away with the idea of a free consultation. Prospects that are not sure they need your services are not easily convinced.

A better idea for your offer might be a booklet to help them organize their kitchen, a closet cleaning tips brochure, or an information packet on setting up a bill paying system. These examples are warm eye openers. They are non-confrontational and do not obligate the prospect to anything. The best part is…it is complimentary. Consider the effect it may have on a prospect that is not convinced they need your services. They read your ad offering your free booklet or information packet, and all they need to do is send an email or make a phone call requesting it.

Right away, you have created a non-committed environment, and their fears, whatever they may be, become slightly diminished. Automatically, they have opened the door a crack toward trusting you. Once you have peaked their interest, it is critical for you to get your complimentary item sent to your prospect in a timely manner. Later, you may follow up with them after you have given them time to read or view your material.

If you are knowledgeable about organizing methods and have some good ideas, and you have a computer with Internet access, you can easily create a booklet full of helpful information. Some other ideas might be a mini-CD full of organizing tips, or an information packet. Once you have created and designed a good offer, you can use it continuously, provided it is not a seasonal offer such as "101 Tips for Organizing Christmas Decorations."

Making Your Offer Known

Once you have established your offer, the next step is to decide how you are going to deliver it to the public. Your method of advertising is simply the way you get your information to your audience, and let them know what you are offering.

Some methods are free or relatively inexpensive, and others can be very costly. Some require very little investment of time, and others require a considerable amount of time to create and maintain. Some will yield great results, while others may target the wrong people.

Whatever method of marketing you use, you should never choose just one method and rely upon that alone. You have to combine various marketing efforts in order to saturate more of your target audience.

Here is a partial list of marketing methods you can use: (some marketing methods will be explained in further detail)

- Newspaper and magazine ads
- Church bulletin and calendar ads
- Yellow page ads
- Web site ads
- Written articles
- Business cards and brochures
- Flyers on bulletin boards and displays
- Email solicitations
- Fax solicitations
- Web site (owned and operated by you)
- Newsletter subscriptions (created and maintained by you)
- Direct mail letters or coupons
- Flyers for parking lots and doorknob hangers
- TV, radio, newspaper interviews and articles
- News releases
- TV and radio commercials
- Cold call telemarketing
- Referrals (or maybe a discount to customers in a "referral program")
- Trade show booths
- Seminars and workshops
- Billboards
- Magnets/calendars/pens/pads of paper, etc. (free handouts)
- Magnetic signs on your vehicle(s)

> **FREE "CLUTTER CUTTER" TIPS BOOKLET**
> Request your FREE Tips Booklet today!
> Filled with over 100 tips to help Eliminate the clutter in your home!
> **Ask for offer # 22**
> Call or email today, or visit our website at:
> **www.cluttercutter.com**

Regardless of the marketing method you use, you want to make sure you include the following information:

- Your offer and a short description of it
- Who your offer is for
- Methods of response (email, call, mail, fax, etc.)
- Encouragement to act immediately ("for a limited time" or "call today")
- A non-commitment statement ("no obligation")

When a prospect contacts you, it is very important to obtain two pieces of information. First, get their contact information (name, address, phone number, and email address). Second, ask them how they learned about you. Asking this second question is important, because it will help you track the results of your various marketing methods. If you prefer a less direct approach to tracking how prospects and customers hear about your services, you may create a special code, which will allow you to know where the individual learned of your offer (as seen on the sample ad on the previous page, "Ask for offer #22"). If you use a different code for each marketing vehicle, it is relatively easy to track.

To facilitate a trusting and respectable business relationship, it is advisable for you to send the prospect the offer within two business days. Once you send them your offer, you will want to include them in your prospect database or on your prospect list. Begin building a business relationship with that person by contacting them after they have time to look over the information you give them.

Newspaper and Magazine Advertisements

When you advertise in printed media, you can select a variety of different size ads, and a variety of different places to advertise. You can also advertise in local papers or magazines, or national publications.

Regardless of the geographical scope of the printed media, choose the type that targets your ideal audience the best. For example, if you are specializing in working solely with businesses, you should place your ad in a newspaper or magazine that caters mostly to businesses.

If possible, place your ad in the best section of the newspaper or magazine. Just putting an ad in the classifieds is not always enough – it disappears among the hundreds of other ads. Make it stand out by putting it in the "home improvement" section, or the "lifestyles" section, if possible. Just remember to use more than one marketing vehicle, and keep your marketing options open to other ideas if necessary.

Regardless of the size of your ad, there are some components that you should be sure to include. They are:

Headline: This belongs at the top of the ad, and it should clearly state your offer or "jump" out at the reader. Make it interesting, short, and to the point.

Body: Highlight the specifics that are important or key points for the reader to know in line-by-line format or bullet format. Again, be short and specific, and concentrate on what the reader will want or appreciate knowing. Keep it easy to read. Do not use text over graphics, or a busy background that distracts from the ad or makes it difficult to read. Simple is always better.

Contact: Tell the reader how to get the offer, and who they are getting it from. Some companies exclude the company name, or just say, "Contact Mr. Smith." Excluding the company name sends a negative message to the reader that the ad is not a legitimate offer.

Phone Book Advertisements

Becoming a professional organizer is a more popular career, thanks to television programs on cable networks. Depending on your competition, your local phone book may not have a separate category for professional organizers. A benefit to placing a phone book advertisement is that most publishers of the phone book put the information on their Internet directory search site. It increases your exposure, even if it may not generate a considerable number of responses immediately.

If someone is seeking a professional organizer, they will most likely begin their search by looking for one in the yellow pages or online. Phone book advertising is also beneficial because one of your existing clients may refer a friend who only remembers your name. As long as they have your name or your business name, they can look you up in the white or yellow pages (based on where you decide to have your listing). It also helps your business appear more legitimate to your prospects when they can find you in the local directory. It is just common sense to be listed there.

When you run a phone book ad, most companies require a one-year commitment, since most phone books are only printed once a year.

The type of ad you run in the phone book depends entirely upon the amount of money you can afford to spend, and the size of your competitor's ads (if any). If possible, you want to run an ad larger than your competition. The reason for this is when prospects look through the phone book they usually look at the largest ads first. You usually have some flexibility on creating your ad, and you may choose between a single line ad, a boxed ad, or a display ad. It should be located under an appropriate category listing such as "organizing services."

Church or Community Advertisements

Many churches sell space for advertisements in their bulletins, newsletters, yearly calendars and programs for special events. Quite often, these types of organizations accept business card or half-business card size ads. This is a great place to advertise, as many churchgoers prefer to do business with another member of their church, before they look elsewhere for someone to provide the service.

In addition to gaining public exposure with people of similar interests, (religious beliefs, etc.) you will usually be contributing money by paying for your ad to a charitable organization that could greatly benefit from it. The costs for these types of ads are relatively inexpensive.

Aside from printed ads for community organizations, contributing time or supplies to an event, such as a Church Supper can bring some added exposure. If you donate food for an event, the organization will usually display a sign or note in a program or bulletin that gives credit to you for the contribution. You are accomplishing two goals this way, making your business name more known and benefiting a charitable event.

In the business of banking, there is an act known as the Community Reinvestment Act. The principle idea of this Act is to ensure that banks contribute back to the community that they are a part of – the city or town that allows the bank to be in business. Although there is not an Act such as this for other businesses, the principle is a good one. You are a better citizen to a city or town in which you do business when you contribute your time, efforts and talent to the community as a whole, rather than just expecting to profit from it.

Web Site Advertisements

Electronic media, such as newsletters and web sites are great places to advertise. Many newsletter and website owners sell space for advertising, and will also place a link to your home page on their website, provided you do the same. (You scratch my back, I'll scratch yours.)

These types of ads can be text or banner/graphic ads. If you select this method of advertising, make sure the website or newsletter you advertise with has considerable distribution or web traffic, if you will be paying for the ad.
In general, you can expect one to ten percent response from local viewers to your ad.

Writing Your Own Articles

If your writing skills are good, writing an article for a newspaper or magazine can be a great and inexpensive way to advertise. Editors and owners are always on the lookout for a good article. Some types of media you can submit your articles to include newspapers, magazines, websites and electronic newsletters. You can easily submit the same article to a number of media types.

Another advantage to writing articles is that sometimes you are paid for them. The disadvantage to this is you lose the right to sell the article, or share them with other publications, so consider the amount of money you ask for the article before you sell it.

You can submit your articles to publications and inform them that they can print it free of charge provided they include your "resource box." Your resource box can basically be a short advertisement, with your name and company, and a short line such as "Contact ABC Company at (phone number) for 101 Tips to Office Organizing."

Articles Written About You

If you can get a newspaper, magazine, or other publication to write an article about you and your business, the opportunity to generate new prospects is considerable.

If possible, ask the writer of the article to include details of your current offer and a phone number the public may contact you through. Some writers will refuse to include your offer, so at minimum, ask for your website or phone number to be included. At least you will get some exposure, and readers will have a method of contacting you if they are seeking further information.

Before you meet with the writer of the article, it is advisable that you plan ahead and write some notes about yourself and your business that will be interesting. You want to be completely prepared for the interview. Be careful about what you say during the interview, as media interviewers can twist and turn stories away from the perspective you were telling it from, which could ultimately cause you to burn a few bridges behind you.

Advertising Flyers & Signs

Post your flyers in areas of high traffic, such as on bulletin boards, in shop windows, restaurants, or any other place where prospects will see them. Make sure you check with the owner or manager of the business to determine if they permit posting your flyer. You may also decide to hand your flyers out to customers as they enter or exit the business. If you choose this type of advertising, know that many businesses forbid solicitation of their customers or employees, and may ask you to leave.

One large advantage to creating flyers is you have all the space you want. You should design it well and describe your offer thoroughly. Avoid blank or wasted space on your flyers, but keep it from appearing too busy. Customizable ad signs titled *Ad – Sign – Level Theme* (Appendix A, Form 6) and *Ad – Sign – Tear Off Strips* (Appendix A, Form 7) are included in this book.

Direct Mail

Addresses for direct mail can be purchased from direct mail companies. The direct mail companies categorize their lists according to demographic information (homeowners, age groups, homes with children, etc). The prices for mailing lists vary depending on the demographics and the company you purchase it from. The price ranges from five-cents per name to one-dollar per name.

If you want to save money, you can create your own list directly from the local phone book, but you will not have the luxury of selecting your own demographic information.

When you select direct mail, you can either mail first or third class. Third class takes more work than first class, and you will have to follow very strict rules for putting your envelopes together, but it can be less expensive than first class. You should determine the amount of work, compared to the cost savings, and select the choice best for you.

Direct Mail Flyers are easy to create with the help of a mass mailer, such as Valpak®. They will help you create your ad, and can select demographic information for you, much the same as a mail marketing firm does with address lists. For more information about using Valpak® for advertising, visit the website at: www.valpak.com.

Doorknob Hangers

Doorknob hangers are a very inexpensive way of marketing your business. You create a flyer that hangs on doorknobs, and place them at homes around your community. A very important detail that you must remember is that doorknob hangers must go on doorknobs. It is a federal offense to place them inside mailboxes unless you are a postal carrier.

A doorknob hanger template called *Ad – Doorknob Hanger* that you can customize with your computer can be found in Appendix A, Form 2.

Email Spam

I do not recommend doing any form of email Spam. Sending unsolicited bulk email to strangers is not appreciated by people, and will likely give you a poor reputation and many burned bridges. Only contact people by email that have requested it, such as people that sign up for electronic newsletters or tips by email. Always give people the option of opting out of your electronic newsletters or email tips by putting specific instructions on the bottom of the newsletter or email.

Newsletters

If you are creative in your writing ability, you can generate your own newsletters. Newsletters are great marketing tools, because they help you keep in touch with current and potential customers in a non-threatening way. They also build positive relationships, educate customers about your service, and position you as an expert in your field. Ultimately, this helps to increase your sales.

The great thing about newsletters is they can be done very inexpensively and still be successful. A newsletter can be as simple as a one-page black and white printed publication, or as complicated as a multi-color, multi-page electronic publication.

To begin, I recommend you start simple. Your first considerations are content and format of your newsletter. Length is not as important as the content itself. As long as it includes a delightful mix of timely, helpful and interesting information, the newsletter is bound to be a success.

Some ideas I would recommend for your newsletter are:

Customer profiles or success stories: These show off your business with positive customer testimonials or quotes, and before and after pictures (with your customer's approval of course) are great additions.

How-to and feature articles: Give your customers practical and helpful information, which will help to promote their loyalty.

Product information: When you find a new product, brag about it. Write your own "review" of that product, and give tips for using it and tell your customers where they can get it. If you create a new product yourself, this is a great way to introduce your customers to it.

Industry trends, research and findings: Inform your customers on the latest, cutting edge information.

Response tools: Entice your customers with a giveaway, contest, or coupons.

Customer support: Host a Q & A column or a "10 tips for…" column.

Site of the week: Let customers know about websites you have found that are helpful or informative.

Be creative! Once you know what types of articles you would like to feature, write and create your newsletter. As an expert in your field, you can probably write some very informative and interesting articles all by yourself. If you need some help, you can search trade publications or newspapers for article ideas and research for your newsletter. Note that if you reprint an entire article word for word from a website or publication, you need to obtain permission to avoid copyright infringement!

Once the content is completed, you need a format. Usually a two or three-column format is the easiest to work with, and you can use column formatting in just about any word processing program. Stay away from one big long column; it is just too difficult to read. Use standard fonts, like Times New Roman or Arial and a 12-point type for easy readability. If you know you are catering to some older people, using a 14-point font might be a nice personal touch as well.

Try to balance the text and graphics in your newsletter, and avoid using a lot of small graphics. It is best to stick to one larger graphic for each page than many small ones. It is just more appealing to the eye.

Your headlines can be a different font size and bolded to make them stand out. Do not forget to give your newsletter a snappy name that will make readers want to read it.

You can distribute your newsletter by email, posting it on your website, and/or mailing a physical copy of it. If you mail a physical copy, I highly recommend using Kinko's® or some other copy place to make photocopies. Printing all the copies yourself by computer can be cost-prohibitive, especially if your mailing list is lengthy.

Most importantly, remember that your newsletter is a direct reflection of your business and your knowledge as a professional organizer. It is very important to proofread your articles and check it for errors. Make it perfect!

Do not sell advertising space in your newsletter or load it chock-full of your own publicity offers. Place an enticing offer in your newsletter in one place, and stick to other content from there.

Do not solicit prospects or customers by sending your newsletter to them without their permission; this is just a courtesy to them. You can advertise your newsletter on your website and ask people to email you if they want to sign up for it, and you can ask customers if they would like to be included on your mailing list. Newsletter templates titled *Newsletter – Aztec, Newsletter – Email* and *Newsletter – Professional* can be found in Appendix A, Forms 48 to 50.

News Releases

The media is always looking for content for their audience, and by making an effective news release, you can get your message out for little, or no cost at all.

News releases are not advertisements. If you write a news release to sound like an advertisement, the media will probably not use it. You have to make it an interesting story, offer, free service or product for the public. Remember that the media is not obligated to print your news release. They will only use it if they feel it will benefit their audience, and if they have room for it.

When you create a news release, you need to define the five "W's." They are:

- Who
- What
- When
- Where
- Why

You should try to get the five "W's" covered within the first sentence or first two sentences if possible. The media provides information in a backwards manner compared to writing a typical story. All the questions are answered right away in the article or story. A person could read the first few sentences, and know all the basics. Keep this in mind when you are creating your news release.

It is important to target the correct department editor when sending your news release. If you are sending it to a large media source, send it to the attention of the business editor or lifestyles editor. By doing this, you have a greater chance of it getting read compared to just sending it to the "editor." Remember that the media has no obligation to print or announce your news release. Avoid annoying the editor or the customer service department by calling and sending letters asking if your news release has been used. If you annoy them, your news release may end up in the trash rather than in the news.

A *News Release Worksheet* that can be used to create your own news release can be found in Appendix A, Form 47. There are two sample news releases, *News Release - Elegant* (Appendix A, Form 45) and *News Release - Professional* (Appendix A, Form 46).

Chapter 6

6: Generating Customers

Getting Responses

Once you have an effective offer and you market that offer, you will begin to receive responses from prospects. This is the beginning of building lasting business relationships.

As you receive phone calls and make follow up calls, if your prospects are friendly and talkative, take the time to talk with them. Listen to their needs, ask questions, give them some helpful tips, and work toward building a friendly rapport with them.

Make sure you write down information as they provide it to you, even some of the most discreet information, such as telling you in passing that their bedroom closet is a disaster. You should note that is an area of concern for them, or they would not have mentioned it. The little details provided during this phase of establishing a trusting relationship, can make a big difference down the road. If you note this information on scrap paper, or if you use a *Prospect Data Sheet* (Appendix A, Form 55), be sure to transfer it to your prospect database (if you have one).

Make sure you send the prospect your offer within two business days. It is poor business practice to wait to send it any longer. When you mail the offer to the prospect, include your business card and details about your services. A brochure is a great way to get this information across. Once you mail the information, note it in your prospect database and on your calendar to follow up, along with your method for contacting them (telephone, email, etc.).

Your Follow Up

Moving someone from a prospect to a customer can be an experience that takes time and skill. Some individuals are not successful sales people because they cannot ask for the sale, which shows that you can work really hard to get there, but end up losing in the end by missing a crucial step. Many people are afraid to ask for the sale because they are afraid of being rejected. Many employees at the bank ran into this same problem. They did not know how to handle rejection and could not overcome customer's objections.

Making follow-up calls is one of the most effective ways for you to get your foot in the door, especially when you have already sent the prospect some literature and they know you exist. Some individuals send letters or cards to follow up with a prospect rather than making a phone call. A phone call is a much more personal and effective method of following up. When you do a follow-up call, know what you are going to say. If you have ever heard telemarketers, they usually sound like everything they are saying is scripted. This is the number one follow-up mistake! Do your homework. Write down possible objections, and reasonable responses to overcome them. Ask your spouse or friend to work with you so you can practice handling objections. Get comfortable communicating about your services and get used to rejection, and learn to overcome it.

Below are a few examples of common objections and possible responses to them:

> **Rejection:** I just do not have the time to spend getting this organized.
>
> **Response:** *I understand and respect your position, especially when you have children and are working a full time job. It can be exhausting just figuring out what to do next, much less getting it done! I realize you may not be prepared to set aside some time for this now, but please keep in mind that the time you invest when you are ready to tackle this project will help you save so much time and energy in the future. I also want you to know that I am available to work evenings and weekends, and no matter how long a project will take us, we can break it up into multiple smaller sessions so it doesn't become too time consuming and too overwhelming. Do you mind if I check back with you next week and we can see if you will have an evening or weekend that I can come do a free evaluation and see exactly how long it would take to get it done?*
>
> **Rejection:** I do not think I need help with it. I just need to sit down and actually do it.
>
> **Response:** *Mary, how long have you been putting this off for? My point is, sometimes, we all need a little motivation and most of all, a second perspective on things. Maybe you have avoided doing it because you aren't sure what to keep and what to get rid of. I specialize in helping you work through that. Together, we can sit down, go through it all, and make rational decisions as to what stays and what goes. Then we can put a plan together to help you keep it organized forever! It only takes a little time for me to do a free consultation, and then we can discuss what we are realistically looking at in terms of time and effort to complete it.*

Realize that it may take anywhere from one to twelve follow-up calls to get an appointment with a prospect. If you cannot get an appointment by then, you have likely overestimated the prospects interest.

Remember to use tact, and saying, "Are you ready to buy yet?" is not using tact. It only takes one occurrence of saying the wrong thing to lose a prospect forever. Make sure that when you call, you are calling for a purpose. Just calling to "see how everything is going" makes the prospect feel like you are wasting his or her time. Be sure to offer them something when you call to make it worthwhile.

Free Consultations

An important step in building your business and generating customers is to offer your prospects a free consultation or needs analysis. It is such an important part because it allows you to become familiar with your prospects problem, and determine what solutions you can devise, as well as give them the opportunity to get to know and trust you. Your consultations should never be a fee-based service. You would not ask a salesman to come into your home and charge you for their time when they give you a sales presentation. It is the same for an organizing consultation.

I have moved many times, and one thing that always irritated me was not being able to have a quote from the moving company over the phone. They had to come to my home, look at my stuff, and then give me a quote. So naturally, you would think that I would be an advocate for doing a phone consultation for your customers. Surprisingly, I am not.

The best way for you to get an idea of the amount of time, effort and supplies required to get a job done, will be to assess the situation in person. I can describe my desk to you, and the current condition of it, but until you actually see it, you do not really get a clear picture. It is like my mother's "organized mess." To her, it is all in neat little piles, according to category and type. To me, it is a mountain of stacked papers and scribbled notes with no semblance of order or organization. It is all perspective.

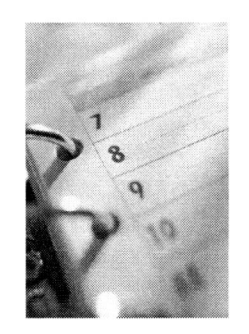

The Appointment

When you meet or speak to a prospect about a project, it is very important for you to do everything within your power to help the potential customer feel comfortable. Start with friendly chatter, or something personal like how lovely their home is, or how you like the neighborhood they live in.

Many people are not comfortable with strangers being in their house, especially when the whole purpose for you being there is to assess their mess. It is not uncommon for your prospects to say, "Please excuse my mess." This would be a great time to tell them, "Please do not worry about it, that is why I am here, to help. It really isn't as overwhelming as it may seem to you now."

Another important thing to keep in mind is your customer's confidentiality. You are in their home or their business. What you see may be very sensitive and confidential in nature. You should treat it as such and ease their fears if the subject ever comes up. Let them know that you are there to help them find order to the confusion, and will hold whatever documents or information you see in strict confidence. Do not just say it – do it!

Assessing The Project

When you conduct an initial consultation, you have a few goals to accomplish. As I mentioned earlier, you always want to make your prospect feel comfortable and at ease. The next thing you need to accomplish is to assess the situation. Look at the project the prospect wants to work on the most. Do not jump in too far too fast. If your potential client has five different areas to work on, take one at a time, and assess it separately from the others. This prevents you and the prospect from becoming overwhelmed.

The next step is to offer a solution that your customer will be excited about. You want to make the offer enticing; it should be hard to resist your services. Avoid the instinct to view the initial meeting as a sales pitch. A sales pitch can be intimidating and irritating. Try to look at it from the perspective that you are helping your customers. Your responsibility is to help your clients get organized and make some lasting changes in their disorganized life.

Before you quote a price for your services and begin writing a proposal, take the time to determine exactly what your prospect needs. Remember that you are the expert. Listen to their desires and needs, ask questions to clarify things you are not sure about, and remember that your client wants to know what you are thinking. Be careful not to say things like, "Wow, this is a huge project," or "Dang, we sure have our work cut out for us, don't we?" This is more of an insult to your client, and will turn them away from your services.

As you assess the project, determine how to organize a particular space, and concentrate on how it got that way. The root of the problem is often hidden, and you have to look for it in underlying places. Ask yourself; is it their organizational system, are they just plain messy, or is it a time constraint issue? Try to understand the root of the problem and solve that along with the problem itself. It is wonderful if you can organize someone, but if they cannot keep the system going after you leave, then it is ineffective, and ultimately, not worth their time and money to do again.

Remember to close the deal by asking for the appointment. A good way to do this would be to say, "What day would work best for you to begin? Do you want to do this in one session, or would you rather break it up into smaller sessions?" At this point, if the prospect is not convinced they need you, they will let you know. This is not necessarily a permanent decision on the prospects part. There are many factors that may prevent them from hiring you right away. Perhaps it is financial, time management, or they just are not convinced of their need for your services. Be sure they do not want your services before you hastily forget about them and cross their name off your prospect list.

Make sure you have a *Needs Assessment* form with you (Appendix A, Form 44), so you can jot down notes and ideas, as well as things the customer informs you of that are important to them. Sketches and measurements are helpful as well, depending on the project. The more information you obtain in the beginning, the easier it will be for you to design an appropriate plan of action and create a formal proposal (if necessary).

Proposals

Some businesses need to have the organizing expense approved by a department head or accounting office. For this purpose, I recommend creating a formal proposal for all businesses. To create a formal proposal, simply type the information on the *Proposal Worksheet* (Appendix A, Form 54) in an organized and easy-to-read fashion. (A sample titled *Proposal – Outline Format* is located in Appendix A, Form 52.)

You do not need to write a formal proposal in all situations. Residential customers are not objectionable to a hand-written proposal for most projects. However, when they have a large project to complete, you should take the information back to your office, devise a plan of action, and then create a formal proposal.

An easy way to offer a proposal immediately is to have preprinted proposals with you. A sample *Proposal Worksheet* along with the *Proposal - Terms and Conditions* that should be on the back of all of your proposals are on the next two pages. The templates for these are located in Appendix A, Forms 54 and 53. Creating a proposal during the initial consultation is more effective because you have the opportunity to effectively handle your prospects objections and discuss alternate options.

Writing A Proposal

It does not have to be perfect, and most certainly does not need to be reinvented with every new prospect. It just needs some simple components:

- **Summarize your goal.** In just a few sentences, tell the prospect what you hope to accomplish.

- **Define the problem.** List the problems that need to be addressed. Be careful not to be too specific, and yet be informative enough to make it clear.

- **Proofread it.** Like a resume, a proposal that has spelling errors or redundant words is unprofessional and it diminishes your credibility.

- **Keep it short and simple.** You do not need to create a ten-page proposal. It would be too overwhelming for your prospect.

- **Make space for signatures.** You should have a space for the prospect to sign and date, as well as for you to sign and date.

Proposal Worksheet

Name: _____ Date: _____

Detailed Problem Areas:
1.
2.
3.
4.
5.
6.

> List the problem areas on the proposal worksheet clearly and specifically.

Detailed Recommended Solutions:
1.
2.
3.
4.
5.
6.

> List the solutions you recommend for fixing the areas listed above. Be clear and specific.

Recommended Products:
1.
2.
3.
4.
5.
6.

> If organizing products or supplies are needed that the customer will keep, list them here.

Complimentary Additions:
1.
2.
3.

> Free handouts, follow-up plans, discounts, etc. can be listed here.

Proposed Price:

Estimated Hours To Complete	
Price Base (labor and personal consultations)	$
Additional Expense (Describe)	$
Additional Expense (Describe)	$
Additional Expense (Describe)	$
Subtotal (Add all columns)	$
Less Discount	- $
Proposed Total Price (Subtotal – Discount)	$

Project Proposal Terms and Conditions

In consideration of the services described in this proposal by Organize My Life!, Client(s) agree to the following terms and conditions:

Payment:

- Client(s) initial paid deposit will be subtracted from the final cost of the project and broken out of each session as described below:

    Session 1:
    Session 2:
    Session 3:

> This should be on the back of your proposal. You should customize it with your company name, and indicate the payment terms. You can find it in Appendix A, Form 53.

- Payment should be made payable to "Organize My Life" and may be made by check, money order, or cash. There will be a charge of $35 for any checks returned for insufficient funds or any bank draft items that are not payable for any reason, as well as additional collection and/or legal fees up to 40% of original project cost in order to compensate for overdraft charges and unpaid account balances. In the event that a Client(s) is unable to pay the initial deposit, it may be waived at the discretion of the Organize My Life! Proprietor, and alternate payment arrangements made, which shall be placed in writing and signed by both proprietor and Client(s).

- Client(s) is responsible for paying for agreed-upon supplies (file folders, labels, storage containers, racks, etc.) necessary for the completion of this project. Organize My Life! will assist Client(s) either by assisting in shopping for the supplies, or in purchasing the supplies for the Client(s). If Organize My Life! purchases supplies on behalf of the Client(s), all supplies will be listed on a Purchase Order form and the Client(s) must sign agreeing to pay the stated amount on the purchase order prior to delivery of the supplies. All supplies must be ordered and delivered to Client(s) home or office prior to the first session date.

- Client(s) is responsible for any travel fees detailed on the reverse of this proposal. Travel fees shall only be incurred if Client(s) is located more than 30 minutes away from Wichita, KS. If travel fees are not listed, none will be incurred.

Schedules/Cancellation Fee:

- Schedules shall be set by verbal mutual agreement between Client(s) and Organize My Life! Professional Organizer(s) at the time of proposal agreement or anytime thereafter.

- Cancellation of a scheduled appointment must be done within 24 hours prior to the date scheduled. Failure to keep any appointment without prior notification OR failure to cancel an appointment within 24 hours prior to the appointment time will be considered a "No Show / Late Cancel" and a fee of $50.00 will be charged; under extenuating emergency circumstances determined by proprietor, this fee may be waived.

- Client(s) is required to be present during organizing sessions and to assist with the projects. It is very important that Client(s) and professional organizer(s) can focus on the session. Therefore, Client(s) must make arrangements for handling incoming phone calls, redirecting visitors, childcare etc. so that sessions are not interrupted.

Performance/Delivery Guarantee:

- Organize My Life! agrees to fulfill the proposed solutions within the amount of time indicated in this proposal, for the proposed price indicated. If Organize My Life! under-estimates the time it takes to do the written proposed project, another session will be added to complete the project. Should this occur, the Client(s) will not be charged more than the original proposed amount.

- Organize My Life! strives to meet a 100% Client(s) satisfaction level. If we failed to meet any of the proposed solutions as detailed in this proposal, provide us within seven business days, a written letter describing what work or parts of the project were not met. Letter should be mailed via return receipt to: 2801 N. Rock Rd., #2004, Wichita, KS 67226. Organize My Life! will then schedule a complimentary session to make necessary adjustments. Failure to make a claim within seven business days implies that you fully accept the completed work at the agreed-upon price.

Turning Down A Job

What happens if you do an initial consultation, and determine that you cannot do the job, or you feel that you cannot help someone?

The best thing for you to do is to tell them right away. The last thing you want is to procrastinate, or tell them you will write up a proposal, and then not follow up with it. This can damage your reputation.

You may be asking yourself, "Why on earth would I turn down a job?" If I ask you to go in and organize my mom's office, and you know she has that "touch my stuff and you're in big trouble" philosophy then I have placed you in an uncomfortable situation, one that you should never undertake. You never want to place yourself in the middle of two or more people that do not agree on the need for your services. You would be better off to turn down the job, and tell the customer that all parties should be on board before you go forward. This takes the heat off from you, and puts the ball in your customer's court.

Another reason I would turn down an offer is if I were asked to organize a basement that was infested with spiders. As much as I hate to admit, spiders are my number one fear in this world. It is irrational, I know, but the reality is, if I took on a project that required me to work in a space where spiders were literally crawling all over the place, I would be doing the customer a disservice. I would be completely ineffective as I sat working through the shivers and chills, just from thoughts of being in close proximity to a spider. You should also refuse to complete a job where your personal safety or health would be at risk. If an area is infested with cockroaches, or a basement is filled with mold that you are allergic to, you would be better off to be honest with the customer and refuse the job, than put your health at risk.

Perhaps you are asked to do a job where you are inexperienced or you have no idea where to begin. You should refer this project to someone with experience in that particular area, and bow out politely, stating you do not have the knowledge and experience necessary to complete the task the way the customer deserves. Sometimes you can refer a job to another professional organizer, and ask to "sit in" on the job, so you can gain some experience. Most professional organizers would not mind the "free" extra hand, and will want to pay you back for the referral in some way.

Guarantees

If you believe in your services and products, and you stand behind what you do 100% then you should offer your customers a guarantee. A guarantee in and of itself will not sell a service or a product, but it will help move the prospect toward a decision with more confidence. They will know with absolute certainty, that if they are not satisfied, you will either refund their money or rectify the matter in some way.

Some examples of common guarantees are:

- 100% Money Back Guarantee (customer is given money back within a specified period of time.)

- Unconditional Satisfaction Guarantee (customer is given additional consultations or organizing sessions free of charge until he or she is satisfied with the project results within a specified period of time.)

- Product Exchange/Refund Guarantee (customer returns product in exchange for another product or refund of money within specified period of time.)

Obviously, you set the standards for the guarantee you offer your customers. Whatever you determine it to be, you should always put it in writing (a good place is on your proposal) and you should discuss the terms with your customer so he or she completely understands.

If the customer ever needs to invoke the guarantee, it is in your best interest to back it up 100% of the time, without argument, until the customer is satisfied that you have done all you can to rectify the situation. You never want to put your reputation on the line by failing to honor a guarantee. My father always said a handshake was as good as a contract in his day. To some people, your word is as good as gold, and they rely upon it to feel comfortable about you as a business owner.

Chapter 7

7: It Is All Business

Customer Types

You will be working with a diverse group of people in your professional organization business. You will be concentrating your efforts on helping them reduce clutter in their homes, organize their lives and time, and setting up systems that work for them. Keep in mind that you are doing more than just helping your customers clean up existing clutter. You are helping them obtain a better quality of life. You are helping them to reduce anxiety and stress, gain some time in their day, and learn a more organized way of living.

It is not enough that you have the talent for organizing. You also need to work well with people. You are in the people business, and the people you will be working with are going to be particular about some areas, and completely irrational in others. You have to be prepared to deal with all kinds of personalities and quirks along the way.

If you are dealing with a packrat, it is not appropriate for you to say, "Look Ms. Smith, you simply have to get over it." If you would not like someone saying that to you, you should not say it to your customer. Treat your customers how you would like to be treated, with respect, dignity and compassion. Understand that some of the clients you will be working with have been harboring their belongings for a long time. Letting go of things that seem useless to you, might be the most difficult hurdle to overcome for them. Have compassion, be understanding, and learn to bargain for what you want to accomplish. The whole idea is that once the clutter is cleaned up, it should stay that way permanently. You do not want them to go right back to being a packrat after you walk out the door (although it would practically guarantee you repeat business, you are not accomplishing your ultimate goal).

To help you understand some of the diverse qualities and personalities you will be working with, I have devised a list of pretend "customers" for you to get to know:

Fred Follower: Fred is the type of personality that would rather follow someone than lead. If you ask him to write something down, he does it immediately. If you ask him to sort something into piles, he does it without reasoning as to why you have asked him to do it this way. If you say something should be donated to charity, he automatically puts it in the charity pile without fighting for it. Fred never asks questions; he never thinks about what you are doing, he is just doing what he is told. Fred is simply a follower.

The difficulty with Fred is that once the project is finished, Fred will go right back to doing things the way he was doing them, because he never learned anything from the experience of de-cluttering his life. He did not reason with what was happening, he just did as he was told. It may seem frustrating to you at first, but you have to understand that Fred is very common in this world. He does not care why or how, he just wants it done. Learn to work with the Fred's of the world, and know that chances are, he will be calling for your services again where you can start over at square one. There is nothing wrong with this type of personality; Fred just does not care how to get to the end result, he just knows he likes it when it is done. Avoid trying to change Fred. You will likely never get him to care much about maintaining the organized lifestyle.

Confused Cathy: Poor Cathy. No matter what you say or how you say it, she just does not have a clue what you are trying to teach her. She tries very hard to understand, but simply is not able to grasp it. She does not know what you are doing, how you are doing it, or even why you are doing things the way you are. She has an extreme desire to learn, but is simply too confused. No matter how well you explain things, or how many times you try to help her understand, sometimes you have to give in to the fight and come to terms with the fact that she may never get it. Get her as organized as you can, and set up a continuation plan so you can try to keep her on track. Let her know that it is okay if she does not get it right away. Eventually, things will start to make sense, but it will have to happen in her time and in her own way.

Sentimental Sarah: Sarah is sensitive and sentimental about every item you sort through. If an object is not a direct sentiment of a date or time or person, it reminds her of one. Being sentimental is a wonderful thing, and it is important to tell Sarah how lovely it is. But you also need to impress upon her how much it is consuming her time and space working around past memories, and not allowing room for the current day to day things that are of equal importance. The worst thing you could do with Sarah, is try to convince her to dump all the things that are sentimental to her. You will only traumatize her. Try to work out a "keep one, donate one" type of system, where she can split the items into two equal piles, one to keep and one to donate. That way she gets to keep the things that are truly sentimental and is able to compromise by letting go of the things that are not as important, although no less sentimental. Make sure that you commend her for being able to let go. It is a big step for her, and she deserves a pat on the back for it.

I Can Do It Ivan: Ivan is a quick learner and a bright man. He watches everything you do with interest and enthusiasm. He wants to learn from you, and clearly understands what you are doing and why you are doing it a certain way. He asks lots of questions about general organization and absorbs every detail he can. Ivan is your "dream customer" because he genuinely cares and works very hard to accomplish the goals you have set. On the other side of the coin, Ivan is probably one customer who will not require repeat services. Once he learns how to organize, he will do the rest on his own, and will have no trouble maintaining it. Ivan would be a great customer to generate referrals from, and he would probably write an excellent testimonial.

Walk-Away Wanda: Wanda is a customer that appreciates what you are doing, but does not think you need much of her help to get it done. She finds every excuse in the book to walk away from the project at hand, and gets involved in other things that have nothing to do with organization. The truth is, Wanda just does not want to do it. She wants someone else to do it for her, and she does not want to be a part of a "team." If you feel the project is one you can handle on your own, then by all means, do it on your own. You may even excuse Wanda and tell her that you can handle it without her assistance. However, if you are working with something that requires her input, you need to insist that she stay focused and help you, or explain that you cannot complete the project and perhaps it would be best to reschedule when she is more willing to work with you.

Hurried Harry: Harry is very excited, and very impatient. He wants the project done yesterday. You simply cannot work fast enough. He is not paying much attention to what you are doing or why, all he cares about is that it gets done – and fast. Harry is not very detail oriented, and does not appreciate that you are. He becomes impatient very quickly and frustrated with tedious tasks. Harry does not like spending considerable time on one area. The best way to work with him is to recognize his personality and explain that for the system to be effective, it must be planned and cannot be rushed. Talk with Harry while doing the project and try to distract his clock-watching. Ask him probing questions that may help him lose track of time and relax. It may be best to work with Harry in multiple sessions that are shorter in nature. If it really becomes a problem then discuss this option with him.

Friendly Francine: Francine is a very nice lady, and is extremely friendly. She loves to talk, and spends considerable time talking to you throughout the project. No matter what you do to redirect her attention to the task at hand, she always finds something to talk about, and it ends up distracting you both from getting the job done. Francine simply cannot stay focused. It is important to try to redirect her attention. Perhaps send her to another room with a drawer to organize or a stack of papers to go through, or even send her into the yard with piles of items to sort. You have to try to get Francine out of the area and in a solitary situation where nothing can distract her. You may choose to tactfully tell Francine that the story sounds interesting, but you both need to concentrate on the task at hand.

Depressed Donald: Donald feels as if he is the most disorganized person on the planet. He is very critical of himself and feels like a complete failure for his situation. Donald appreciates your help, but cannot stop kicking himself every time he turns around. Understand that this is just another personality trait, and reassure him that he is not a failure. Take the time to explain that organization is a learned way of life, and that literally millions of people in the world simply have not been able to learn the most effective way of staying organized. That is, after all, why you are in business! Reassure Donald that he is on the road to an organized lifestyle, and you have every confidence that he can be successful at it. Do what you can to bolster his enthusiasm and let him know that if he needs additional consultation after the final project completion, you are just a phone call away.

I Don't Like It Lana: Lana is possibly an elderly person, who has been doing things her way for a long time. She is very resistant to change, and does not care how much your ideas could benefit her. No matter what you recommend, she disagrees with you, and you discover that you are getting nowhere. Lana's issues are much more than a need to get organized, and in most cases it will be best to tell her that you do not believe the job is working, and refund any of her money and let it be. You simply cannot work against the grain 100% of the time, and with Lana, that is what you would be doing.

Hesitant Helen: Helen is indecisive and afraid of change. If you tell her something can be donated, she puts it to the side and wants to think about it. If you ask her to move something to another location in the room, she hesitates, and resists, stating she needs to think about it. Helen is not resisting you because she does not like your ideas. She is simply afraid of change. Some people accept change well, and some cannot stand change. They get used to things being a certain way, and are comfortable with it. Uprooting their surroundings and moving them all around is only confusing to them and causes them to be uncomfortable in their own home. Work carefully with Helen, and reassure her that it is okay to feel unsure about change. Help her to make small changes, such as rearranging drawers, and gradually work your way up to larger changes such as furniture. Eventually, Helen will either see the difference the change made, or will just want things back the way they used to be. Either way, you can only do so much, and Helen needs to pick up the ball and run with it from there.

Overwhelmed Oscar: Oscar is the kind of person who works for a short period of time, then becomes very flustered and overwhelmed. He cannot bear to work on things for any length of time, and only sees the project as one big headache that will never go away. The only thing to do with Oscar is to keep pressing on. Sometimes it might help to distract him to make the time go faster, then bring him back to reality by helping him see how much you have accomplished. He needs to know that the problem is not as bad as it seems to be, and if you take it one step at a time, there is no such thing as a project too large to tackle.

Undesirable Situations

From time to time, you may run into situations that are undesirable. I have already touched on two of the most common, but want to revisit them and clarify how you should handle them if they arise.

Every now and then, you may have a client with a house that is infested with rodents or bugs. Perhaps you are allergic to her dog, or the house has a smell that you simply cannot stand to work around. There is nothing that says you have to work with every client.

Perhaps you have a person who does not want your services but felt pressured into it by relatives or an employer. Perhaps the house is in a horrible state of disrepair or the neighborhood is in a high crime area.

All of these situations are ones in which you would be better off to walk away. You should return any money paid by the customer, explain that you cannot help them, and leave. No amount of money is as important as your health or ability to be comfortable and safe. It just is not worth it.

Repeat Sales

Once you turn a prospect into a customer, and have completed a project for them, it is time for you to see what other services your customer could benefit from. What else do you have that they may be interested in? Perhaps they have multiple areas in their home or office that could use organizing? How can you add to the first sale and get repeat business? It is much easier to sell to someone who has already worked with you because you have already built a rapport with him or her. They trust you. They know the kind of work that you do, and appreciate the help you have already given them.

Keep in touch with your customers regularly. Many professional organizers create a newsletter. Send customers articles you feel would benefit them and add them to your holiday card list. Basically, make them feel like they are one of your special customers. If you offer a special discount or coupon, be sure to include them.

Even if you cannot turn your customers into lifelong clients, they can become your best advocates. If you do something for someone who appreciates it and are thrilled with your expertise, they will tell everyone they know about you. Make your advocates feel special by giving them free services once in a while, and they may generate more business for you than you imagined. Some advocates are better than the best ad you can place in the media, and you will benefit in the long run by making them want to refer you!

Continuation Plans

If at the end of your first session with a customer, you feel they need regular assistance, you should recommend a continuation plan. Basically, this is a plan in which you return to the customer's home or office every month or every quarter, etc., to help him or her reduce the clutter, reorganize, and get back on track.

You should always give someone on a continuation plan a considerable discount – for example 50% off your normal regular hourly rate, provided they contract with you for a specified period of time. This will help your customers become "repeat customers" and stay organized. It will also bring you more steady income without needing to advertise.

Not all customers on continuation plans become lifelong customers, but they can easily become advocates when they realize all you have done to help them make the system work.

Building Your Credentials

The best promotional tool you can have is a collection of testimonials, articles you have written, before and after photographs and case studies of various projects in a portfolio. Get a nice 3-ring binder with some sheet protectors, and create a record of your work history. Keep in mind that your portfolio should tell a story; it is really your resume. Keep it updated, and take it with you whenever you visit a prospect or client in case they ask for credentials or in case you want to show them an example of a previous job you have done.

Testimonials: It is relatively easy to get customer testimonials. You can give them a form upon completion of a job and ask them to fill it out for you before you leave. I have included some sample forms titled *Customer Survey – Quality Scale* (Appendix A, Form 30) and *Customer Survey – Testimonial* (Appendix A, Form 31). Sometimes, a short one-sentence testimonial is all you need. If a customer says something like, "Thank you for organizing my closet, I just can't believe the difference!" ask them if you can use their statement as a testimonial, write it on a piece of paper, and ask them to sign it. That is all it takes. Sometimes customers send you thank you cards or letters complimenting or thanking you for your services. Include these items in your binder to help build your credentials.

Before and After Pictures: Before and after pictures should be a standard practice for you. It is ideal if you use a digital camera, but even a disposable one will do. Take pictures of the area you will be working on before you begin, and then again after completion. (It is always wise to ask the customer for permission before taking pictures.) You can use the pictures to create self-explanatory visuals of your expertise. You may want to make a copy for your customer to show the results of the project, and help convince them to do other areas.

Case Studies: Case studies are notes you type listing the problems and solutions to a project you have completed. They should be included in your portfolio. Photographs are excellent additions to case studies.

Conclusion

Now that you have learned all about starting, operating and marketing your professional organizing business, it is time for you to get started! Think about your personal objectives and the topics I have covered in this book. Add your own personal touch, and strive to reach your goal of being a successful professional organizer.

You have all the tools you need to do what you have always wanted to do, so go out and let your natural talent for organizing shine!

Appendix A: Forms

All the forms that are shown in this appendix are also located on the companion Forms CD, with the same form number and file name. You may customize the forms on the CD for your individual business needs.

Disclaimer: The author and publisher of this book and the corresponding forms make no claims or warranties of any kind as to the accuracy or content of the documents contained herein.

Form Number	File Name	Form Number	File Name
1	Ad - Coupon	31	Customer Survey - Testimonial
2	Ad - Doorknob Hanger	32	Fax Cover - Professional
3	Ad - Gift Certificates	33	Invoice - Product
4	Ad - Pocket Reference	34	Invoice - Service
5	Ad - Postcards - Special Offer	35	Invoice - Time Tracking
6	Ad - Sign - Level Theme	36	Label - Date Tab - Multicolor
7	Ad - Sign - Tear Off Strips	37	Label - Date Tab - Solid
8	Articles of Incorporation	38	Label - Full Color
9	Brochure - Catalog - Geometric	39	Label - Letter Tab - Multicolor
10	Brochure - Catalog - Professional	40	Label - Letter Tab - Solid
11	Brochure - Trifold - Adventure	41	Label - Project Name
12	Brochure - Trifold - Level	42	Label - Task Oriented
13	Brochure - Trifold - Simple	43	Label - Text - White
14	Business Card - Boutique	44	Needs Assessment
15	Business Card - Consulting	45	News Release - Elegant
16	Business Card - Engineering	46	News Release - Professional
17	Business Card - Globe	47	News Release Worksheet
18	Business Card - Level	48	Newsletter - Aztec
19	Business Card - Organize My Life	49	Newsletter - Email
20	Business Card - Simple	50	Newsletter - Professional
21	Calendar - Daily	51	Partnership Agreement
22	Calendar - Monthly	52	Proposal - Outline Format
23	Calendar - Weekly	53	Proposal - Terms and Conditions
24	Calendar - Yearly	54	Proposal Worksheet
25	Collection Letter - NSF Check	55	Prospect Data Sheet
26	Collection Letter - Overdue Account	56	Pruchase Order
27	Collection Letter - Second Reminder	57	Receipts
28	Customer Management List	58	Testimonial - Request To Write
29	Customer Referral List	59	Testimonial - Request To Use
30	Customer Survey - Quality Scale	60	SS4 - Application for EIN *(CD ONLY)*

DISCOUNT COUPON

Receive ONE FREE HOUR OF CONSULTATION.

ORGANIZE MY LIFE!

Redeemable upon signing a proposal for 2 hours minimal paid consultation.
Expires December 31, 2004

www.organize-mylife.com

DISCOUNT COUPON

Receive ONE FREE HOUR OF CONSULTATION.

ORGANIZE MY LIFE!

Redeemable upon signing a proposal for 2 hours minimal paid consultation.
Expires December 31, 2004

www.organize-mylife.com

DISCOUNT COUPON

Receive ONE FREE HOUR OF CONSULTATION.

ORGANIZE MY LIFE!

Redeemable upon signing a proposal for 2 hours minimal paid consultation.
Expires December 31, 2004

www.organize-mylife.com

DISCOUNT COUPON

Receive ONE FREE HOUR OF CONSULTATION.

ORGANIZE MY LIFE!

Redeemable upon signing a proposal for 2 hours minimal paid consultation.
Expires December 31, 2004

www.organize-mylife.com

Cut Along Dotted Line

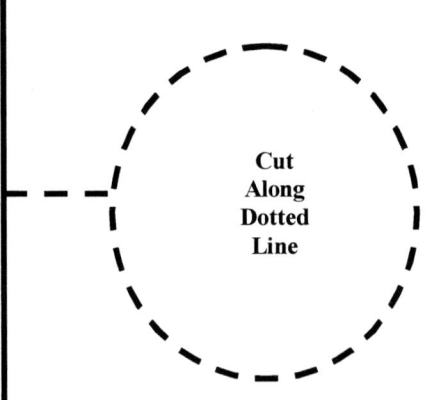

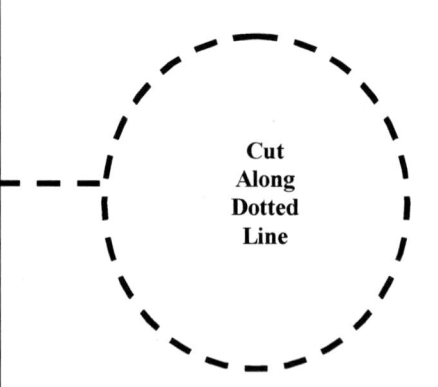

Spring is Here!

Get a jump-start on your spring cleaning with our FREE booklet.

101 Spring Cleaning Tips!

To request your FREE booklet,
call 555-5555
OR
Email your request to:
organizemylife@cox.net

Jamie Smith
Professional Organizer
Serving the Kansas City Area

Cut Along Dotted Line

Spring is Here!

Get a jump-start on your spring cleaning with our FREE booklet.

101 Spring Cleaning Tips!

To request your FREE booklet,
call 555-5555
OR
Email your request to:
organizemylife@cox.net

Jamie Smith
Professional Organizer
Serving the Kansas City Area

Company Name

Gift Certificate

This certificate entitles

To

Business Address
Your Address Line 2
Your Address Line 3
Your Address Line 4

Authorized by

Expires

Not redeemable for cash. Redemption value not to exceed $00.00

Number

Company Name

Gift Certificate

This certificate entitles

To

Business Address
Your Address Line 2
Your Address Line 3
Your Address Line 4

Authorized by

Expires

Not redeemable for cash. Redemption value not to exceed $00.00

Number

Company Name

Gift Certificate

This certificate entitles

To

Business Address
Your Address Line 2
Your Address Line 3
Your Address Line 4

Authorized by

Expires

Not redeemable for cash. Redemption value not to exceed $00.00

Number

© 2006, Lisa Steinbacher, Organize My Life!

Pocket Reference for
Your Project

Providing your audience or team members with a small card to help them remember key points can be a good way to leave a lasting impression. Print this template double-sided on business card stock to make it last longer.

On your pocket reference card you may want to list
- A summary of your message or goal
- The basic points you have made
- Information that is hard to remember such as codes or shortcuts

You can also continue to tell more about your project or presentation on the back side of the card.

(continued on back)

Pocket Reference for
Your Project

Providing your audience or team members with a small card to help them remember key points can be a good way to leave a lasting impression. Print this template double-sided on business card stock to make it last longer.

On your pocket reference card you may want to list
- A summary of your message or goal
- The basic points you have made
- Information that is hard to remember such as codes or shortcuts

You can also continue to tell more about your project or presentation on the back side of the card.

(continued on back)

(The above card design repeats 8 times total on the page, arranged in 2 columns and 4 rows.)

Ad - Pocket Reference (Form 4)

Spring is in the air!
It's the perfect time to Organize Your Life!

Present this card for a 10% discount on our spring organizing services from Organize My Life!
www.organize-mylife.com

Spring is in the air!
It's the perfect time to Organize Your Life!

Present this card for a 10% discount on our spring organizing services from Organize My Life!
www.organize-mylife.com

Spring is in the air!
It's the perfect time to Organize Your Life!

Present this card for a 10% discount on our spring organizing services from Organize My Life!
www.organize-mylife.com

Spring is in the air!
It's the perfect time to Organize Your Life!

Present this card for a 10% discount on our spring organizing services from Organize My Life!
www.organize-mylife.com

Ad - Postcards - Special Offer (Form 5)

Get Organized!

Organize My Life!
Your business tag line here.

Text goes here.

YOUR LOGO HERE

Company Name

Street Address
Address 2
City, ST ZIP Code
Phone: (725) 555-0125
Fax: (725) 555-0145
E-mail address

Ad – Sign – Level Theme (Form 6)

Organize It All!

Get Organized!

List Services and information here!!!!

Name
Address
Telephone number
E-mail address

Name
Address
Telephone number
E-mail address

Name
Address
Telephone number
E-mail address

Name
Address
Telephone number
E-mail address

Name
Address
Telephone number
E-mail address

Name
Address
Telephone number
E-mail address

Name
Address
Telephone number
E-mail address

Name
Address
Telephone number
E-mail address

ARTICLES OF INCORPORATION

Article ONE.

NAME

The name of this corporation is _____.

Article TWO.

OBJECTS AND PURPOSES

The objects and purposes for which this corporation is formed are:

To conduct and transact generally the business of a _____ *[insert type of business]* corporation and to do all things and exercise all powers and perform all functions that a _____ corporation is authorized or empowered to do, exercise, or perform under and by virtue of the laws of _____ *[state]*, or that it may be by law hereafter authorized to do, exercise, or perform; *[list specific functions]* and do all the above things as a _____ corporation and insofar as is consistent with the laws of _____ *[state]*.

Article THREE.

LOCATION OF PRINCIPAL OFFICE

The principal office for the transaction of business of this corporation is to be located in _____ County, _____ *[state]*.

Article FOUR.

REGISTERED AGENT

The registered agent for service of process upon the corporation is:

Name   Address in *[state]*

_____   _____

Article FIVE.

CAPITALIZATION

The total number of shares that the corporation is authorized to issue is _____ shares, and all such shares are to have a par value, and the aggregate par value of all such shares is _____ Dollars ($_____).

Article SIX.

DIRECTORS

The number of directors of the corporation is _____; the following are the names and residences of the persons appointed to act as directors until their successors are elected and qualified:

Names   Residences

_____   _____

_____   _____

_____   _____

Article SEVEN.

DURATION OF CORPORATE EXISTENCE

The corporate existence of this corporation shall continue perpetually.

In witness whereof, we, the incorporators, have set our hands and seals on _____ *[date]*.

[Signatures]

[Seals]

[Acknowledgment]

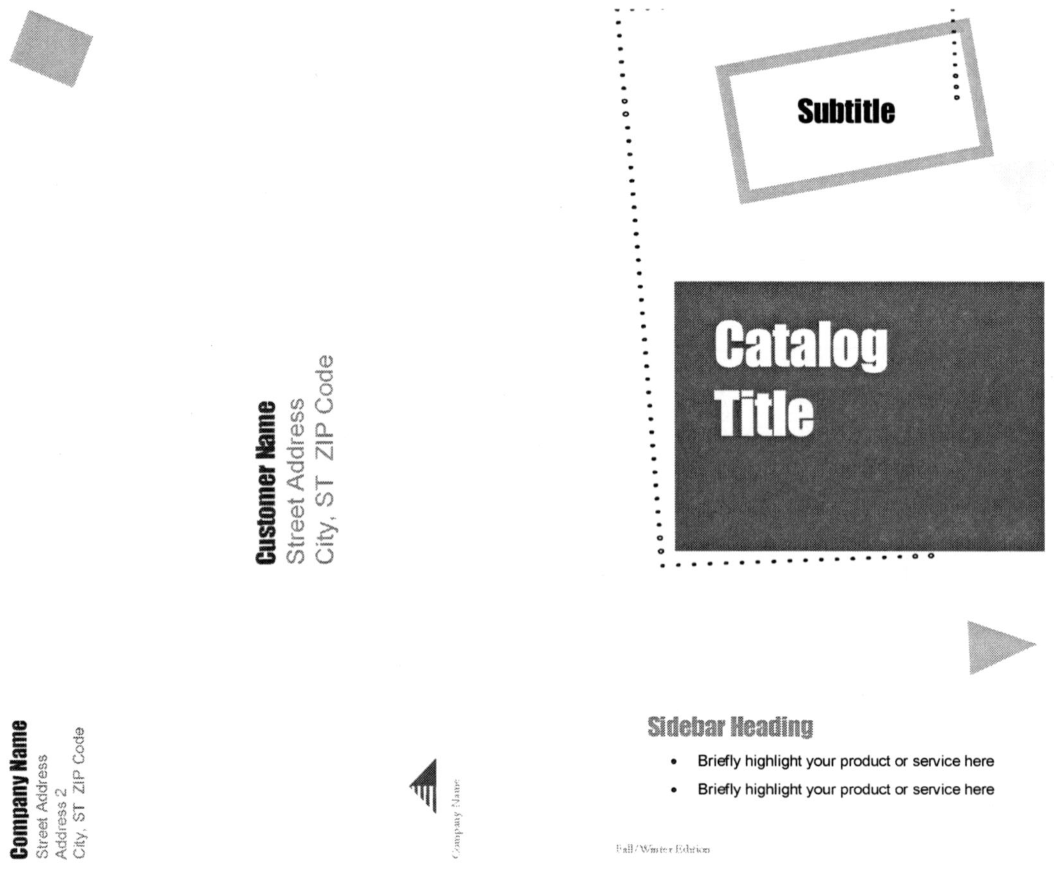

Subtitle

Catalog Title

Sidebar Heading
- Briefly highlight your product or service here
- Briefly highlight your product or service here

Fall/Winter Edition

Customer Name
Street Address
City, ST ZIP Code

Company Name
Street Address
Address 2
City, ST ZIP Code

Company Name

Brochure – Catalog – Geometric (Form 9)

Brochure – Catalog – Professional (Form 10)

Brochure – Trifold – Adventure (Form 11)

Company Name

Product/Service Information

Back Panel Heading

This is a good place to briefly, but effectively, summarize your products or services. Sales copy is typically not included here.

Company Name

Street Address
Address 2
City, ST ZIP Code
Phone: 325.555.0125
Fax: 325.555.0145
E-mail address

YOUR LOGO HERE

Your business tag line here.

Phone: 325.555.0125

Brochure - Trifold - Level (Form 12)

Back Panel Heading

This is a good place to briefly but effectively summarize your products or services. This will entice customers to look more closely at your event.

Mention features of your event that you want to highlight—a special guest, rare opportunity, exclusive offer, etc.

Indicate event location, dates, and registration deadlines to provide the customer with the most critical information about your event.

Provide a description of your company and the products or services that you provide. Reinforce why your special event is important, and why your company is an authority on the topic of the event.

Caption describing picture or graphic.

Brochure - Trifold - Simple (Form 13)

[Company Name]
[Street Address]
[Address 2]
[City, ST ZIP Code]

Address Correction Required

[CUSTOMER NAME]
[STREET ADDRESS]
[ADDRESS 2]
[CITY, ST ZIP CODE]

Type Your Title Here

[Company Name]

Company's tag line

Phone: [Phone number]
Web site: [Web site address]

Brochure – Trifold – Simple (Form 13)

Name of Business
www.business.com

Phone (555) 555-0100
Fax: (555) 555-0199

Name of Business
www.business.com

Phone (555) 555-0100
Fax: (555) 555-0199

Name of Business
www.business.com

Phone (555) 555-0100
Fax: (555) 555-0199

Name of Business
www.business.com

Phone (555) 555-0100
Fax: (555) 555-0199

Name of Business
www.business.com

Phone (555) 555-0100
Fax: (555) 555-0199

Name of Business
www.business.com

Phone (555) 555-0100
Fax: (555) 555-0199

Name of Business
www.business.com

Phone (555) 555-0100
Fax: (555) 555-0199

Name of Business
www.business.com

Phone (555) 555-0100
Fax: (555) 555-0199

Name of Business
www.business.com

Phone (555) 555-0100
Fax: (555) 555-0199

Name of Business
www.business.com

Phone (555) 555-0100
Fax: (555) 555-0199

Business Card - Boutique (Form 14)

Business Card - Consulting (Form 15)

TOM STEPHENS PRINCIPAL ENGINEER	WEST COAST DIVISION 222 EAST VINE STREET SEATTLE, WA 98663 TELEPHONE: (800) 555-5555 FAX: (800) 555-5555 EMAIL: tstephens@eci.com

ENGINEERING CONSULTING INTERNATIONAL

TOM STEPHENS PRINCIPAL ENGINEER	WEST COAST DIVISION 222 EAST VINE STREET SEATTLE, WA 98663 TELEPHONE: (800) 555-5555 FAX: (800) 555-5555 EMAIL: tstephens@eci.com

ENGINEERING CONSULTING INTERNATIONAL

TOM STEPHENS PRINCIPAL ENGINEER	WEST COAST DIVISION 222 EAST VINE STREET SEATTLE, WA 98663 TELEPHONE: (800) 555-5555 FAX: (800) 555-5555 EMAIL: tstephens@eci.com

ENGINEERING CONSULTING INTERNATIONAL

TOM STEPHENS PRINCIPAL ENGINEER	WEST COAST DIVISION 222 EAST VINE STREET SEATTLE, WA 98663 TELEPHONE: (800) 555-5555 FAX: (800) 555-5555 EMAIL: tstephens@eci.com

ENGINEERING CONSULTING INTERNATIONAL

TOM STEPHENS PRINCIPAL ENGINEER	WEST COAST DIVISION 222 EAST VINE STREET SEATTLE, WA 98663 TELEPHONE: (800) 555-5555 FAX: (800) 555-5555 EMAIL: tstephens@eci.com

ENGINEERING CONSULTING INTERNATIONAL

TOM STEPHENS PRINCIPAL ENGINEER	WEST COAST DIVISION 222 EAST VINE STREET SEATTLE, WA 98663 TELEPHONE: (800) 555-5555 FAX: (800) 555-5555 EMAIL: tstephens@eci.com

ENGINEERING CONSULTING INTERNATIONAL

TOM STEPHENS PRINCIPAL ENGINEER	WEST COAST DIVISION 222 EAST VINE STREET SEATTLE, WA 98663 TELEPHONE: (800) 555-5555 FAX: (800) 555-5555 EMAIL: tstephens@eci.com

ENGINEERING CONSULTING INTERNATIONAL

TOM STEPHENS PRINCIPAL ENGINEER	WEST COAST DIVISION 222 EAST VINE STREET SEATTLE, WA 98663 TELEPHONE: (800) 555-5555 FAX: (800) 555-5555 EMAIL: tstephens@eci.com

ENGINEERING CONSULTING INTERNATIONAL

Business Card – Engineering (Form 16)

Name of Business	**Name of Business**
Chris Meyer Position Title 1234 Main Street Glendale, CA 98111 Phone 555.555.0100 Fax 555.555.1100 someone@example.com	**Chris Meyer** Position Title 1234 Main Street Glendale, CA 98111 Phone 555.555.0100 Fax 555.555.1100 someone@example.com
Name of Business	**Name of Business**
Chris Meyer Position Title 1234 Main Street Glendale, CA 98111 Phone 555.555.0100 Fax 555.555.1100 someone@example.com	**Chris Meyer** Position Title 1234 Main Street Glendale, CA 98111 Phone 555.555.0100 Fax 555.555.1100 someone@example.com
Name of Business	**Name of Business**
Chris Meyer Position Title 1234 Main Street Glendale, CA 98111 Phone 555.555.0100 Fax 555.555.1100 someone@example.com	**Chris Meyer** Position Title 1234 Main Street Glendale, CA 98111 Phone 555.555.0100 Fax 555.555.1100 someone@example.com
Name of Business	**Name of Business**
Chris Meyer Position Title 1234 Main Street Glendale, CA 98111 Phone 555.555.0100 Fax 555.555.1100 someone@example.com	**Chris Meyer** Position Title 1234 Main Street Glendale, CA 98111 Phone 555.555.0100 Fax 555.555.1100 someone@example.com
Name of Business	**Name of Business**
Chris Meyer Position Title 1234 Main Street Glendale, CA 98111 Phone 555.555.0100 Fax 555.555.1100 someone@example.com	**Chris Meyer** Position Title 1234 Main Street Glendale, CA 98111 Phone 555.555.0100 Fax 555.555.1100 someone@example.com

Business Card - Globe (Form 17)

Company Name

Street Address
Address 2
City, ST ZIP Code
Phone: 555.555.0125
Fax: 555.555.0145

E-mail address

Employee Name

Position Title

YOUR LOGO
HERE

Company Name

Street Address
Address 2
City, ST ZIP Code
Phone: 555.555.0125
Fax: 555.555.0145

E-mail address

Employee Name

Position Title

YOUR LOGO
HERE

Company Name

Street Address
Address 2
City, ST ZIP Code
Phone: 555.555.0125
Fax: 555.555.0145

E-mail address

Employee Name

Position Title

YOUR LOGO
HERE

Company Name

Street Address
Address 2
City, ST ZIP Code
Phone: 555.555.0125
Fax: 555.555.0145

E-mail address

Employee Name

Position Title

YOUR LOGO
HERE

Company Name

Street Address
Address 2
City, ST ZIP Code
Phone: 555.555.0125
Fax: 555.555.0145

E-mail address

Employee Name

Position Title

YOUR LOGO
HERE

Company Name

Street Address
Address 2
City, ST ZIP Code
Phone: 555.555.0125
Fax: 555.555.0145

E-mail address

Employee Name

Position Title

YOUR LOGO
HERE

Company Name

Street Address
Address 2
City, ST ZIP Code
Phone: 555.555.0125
Fax: 555.555.0145

E-mail address

Employee Name

Position Title

YOUR LOGO
HERE

Company Name

Street Address
Address 2
City, ST ZIP Code
Phone: 555.555.0125
Fax: 555.555.0145

E-mail address

Employee Name

Position Title

YOUR LOGO
HERE

Company Name

Street Address
Address 2
City, ST ZIP Code
Phone: 555.555.0125
Fax: 555.555.0145

E-mail address

Employee Name

Position Title

YOUR LOGO
HERE

Company Name

Street Address
Address 2
City, ST ZIP Code
Phone: 555.555.0125
Fax: 555.555.0145

E-mail address

Employee Name

Position Title

YOUR LOGO
HERE

Business Card - Level (Form 18)

Professional Organizing Inc.

Lisa Smith
Professional Organizer
www.organize-mylife.com

555 N. Main St.   (316) 555-5555
Wichita, KS 67226   Email: organizemylife@cox.net

Professional Organizing Inc.

Lisa Smith
Professional Organizer
www.organize-mylife.com

555 N. Main St.   (316) 555-5555
Wichita, KS 67226   Email: organizemylife@cox.net

Professional Organizing Inc.

Lisa Smith
Professional Organizer
www.organize-mylife.com

555 N. Main St.   (316) 555-5555
Wichita, KS 67226   Email: organizemylife@cox.net

Professional Organizing Inc.

Lisa Smith
Professional Organizer
www.organize-mylife.com

555 N. Main St.   (316) 555-5555
Wichita, KS 67226   Email: organizemylife@cox.net

Professional Organizing Inc.

Lisa Smith
Professional Organizer
www.organize-mylife.com

555 N. Main St.   (316) 555-5555
Wichita, KS 67226   Email: organizemylife@cox.net

Business Card - Organize My Life (Form 19)

Professional Organizing Inc.

Lisa Smith
Professional Organizer
www.organize-mylife.com

555 N. Main St.   (316) 555-5555
Wichita, KS 67226   Email: organizemylife@cox.net

Professional Organizing Inc.

Lisa Smith
Professional Organizer
www.organize-mylife.com

555 N. Main St.   (316) 555-5555
Wichita, KS 67226   Email: organizemylife@cox.net

Professional Organizing Inc.

Lisa Smith
Professional Organizer
www.organize-mylife.com

555 N. Main St.   (316) 555-5555
Wichita, KS 67226   Email: organizemylife@cox.net

Professional Organizing Inc.

Lisa Smith
Professional Organizer
www.organize-mylife.com

555 N. Main St.   (316) 555-5555
Wichita, KS 67226   Email: organizemylife@cox.net

Professional Organizing Inc.

Lisa Smith
Professional Organizer
www.organize-mylife.com

555 N. Main St.   (316) 555-5555
Wichita, KS 67226   Email: organizemylife@cox.net

Humongous Insurance

Medical ♦ Dental ♦ Long-Term Care

ERIC ROTHENBERG
Owner

56 N Walnut Drive, Suite 120, New Orleans, LA 12329
Phone (409) 555-0112   Fax (409) 555-0114
License #M45678

Humongous Insurance

Medical ♦ Dental ♦ Long-Term Care

ERIC ROTHENBERG
Owner

56 N Walnut Drive, Suite 120, New Orleans, LA 12329
Phone (409) 555-0112   Fax (409) 555-0114
License #M45678

Humongous Insurance

Medical ♦ Dental ♦ Long-Term Care

ERIC ROTHENBERG
Owner

56 N Walnut Drive, Suite 120, New Orleans, LA 12329
Phone (409) 555-0112   Fax (409) 555-0114
License #M45678

Humongous Insurance

Medical ♦ Dental ♦ Long-Term Care

ERIC ROTHENBERG
Owner

56 N Walnut Drive, Suite 120, New Orleans, LA 12329
Phone (409) 555-0112   Fax (409) 555-0114
License #M45678

Humongous Insurance

Medical ♦ Dental ♦ Long-Term Care

ERIC ROTHENBERG
Owner

56 N Walnut Drive, Suite 120, New Orleans, LA 12329
Phone (409) 555-0112   Fax (409) 555-0114
License #M45678

Humongous Insurance

Medical ♦ Dental ♦ Long-Term Care

ERIC ROTHENBERG
Owner

56 N Walnut Drive, Suite 120, New Orleans, LA 12329
Phone (409) 555-0112   Fax (409) 555-0114
License #M45678

Humongous Insurance

Medical ♦ Dental ♦ Long-Term Care

ERIC ROTHENBERG
Owner

56 N Walnut Drive, Suite 120, New Orleans, LA 12329
Phone (409) 555-0112   Fax (409) 555-0114
License #M45678

Humongous Insurance

Medical ♦ Dental ♦ Long-Term Care

ERIC ROTHENBERG
Owner

56 N Walnut Drive, Suite 120, New Orleans, LA 12329
Phone (409) 555-0112   Fax (409) 555-0114
License #M45678

Humongous Insurance

Medical ♦ Dental ♦ Long-Term Care

ERIC ROTHENBERG
Owner

56 N Walnut Drive, Suite 120, New Orleans, LA 12329
Phone (409) 555-0112   Fax (409) 555-0114
License #M45678

Humongous Insurance

Medical ♦ Dental ♦ Long-Term Care

ERIC ROTHENBERG
Owner

56 N Walnut Drive, Suite 120, New Orleans, LA 12329
Phone (409) 555-0112   Fax (409) 555-0114
License #M45678

Business Card - Simple (Form 20)

Date:	

Time	Appointment/Task
7:00 AM	
8:00 AM	
9:00 AM	
10:00 AM	
11:00 AM	
12:00 PM	
1:00 PM	
2:00 PM	
3:00 PM	
4:00 PM	
5:00 PM	
6:00 PM	
7:00 PM	
Notes:	

Calendar – Daily (Form 21)

January 2006						
SUNDAY	MONDAY	TUESDAY	WEDNESDAY	THURSDAY	FRIDAY	SATURDAY
1	2	3	4	5	6	7
8	9	10	11	12	13	14
15	16	17	18	19	20	21
22	23	24	25	26	27	28
29	30	31				

Calendar – Monthly (Form 22)

Week of <enter week information here>

Monday				Tuesday	
Number	**Name**			**Name**	**Number**
			8		
			9		
			10		
			11		
			12		
			1		
			2		
			3		
			4		
			5		

Wednesday				Thursday	
Number	**Name**			**Name**	**Number**
			8		
			9		
			10		
			11		
			12		
			1		
			2		
			3		
			4		
			5		

Friday				Saturday/Sunday	
Number	**Name**			**Name**	**Number**
			8		
			9		
			10		
			11		
			12		
			1		
			2		
			3		
			4		
			5		

Calendar – Weekly (Form 23)

2006

JANUARY

S	M	T	W	T	F	S
1	2	3	4	5	6	7
8	9	10	11	12	13	14
15	16	17	18	19	20	21
22	23	24	25	26	27	28
29	30	31				

FEBRUARY

S	M	T	W	T	F	S
			1	2	3	4
5	6	7	8	9	10	11
12	13	14	15	16	17	18
19	20	21	22	23	24	25
26	27	28				

MARCH

S	M	T	W	T	F	S
			1	2	3	4
5	6	7	8	9	10	11
12	13	14	15	16	17	18
19	20	21	22	23	24	25
26	27	28	29	30	31	

APRIL

S	M	T	W	T	F	S
						1
2	3	4	5	6	7	8
9	10	11	12	13	14	15
16	17	18	19	20	21	22
23	24	25	26	27	28	29
30						

MAY

S	M	T	W	T	F	S
	1	2	3	4	5	6
7	8	9	10	11	12	13
14	15	16	17	18	19	20
21	22	23	24	25	26	27

JUNE

S	M	T	W	T	F	S
				1	2	3
4	5	6	7	8	9	10
11	12	13	14	15	16	17
18	19	20	21	22	23	24

Calendar – Yearly (Form 24)

BAD CHECK NOTICE: Notice to check issuer of bank's dishonor of check, with demand for payment

Date _____

Name of issuer _____

Street address _____

City and state _____

You are according to law hereby notified that a check dated _____ *[Date]*, drawn on the _____ Bank of _____ in the amount of _____ dollars ($_____) has been returned unpaid with the notation that payment has been refused because (of insufficient funds) (the drawer does not have an account). Within 10 days from the receipt of this notice, you must pay or tender to _____ (holder) sufficient monies to pay the instrument in full.
You are advised to make your payment at the following address: _____.

_____
[Signature of holder]

Collection Letter – NSF Check (Form 25)

[Debtor's name]
[Street address]
[City, state zip]

[Month day, year]

Re: [Account balance]
   [Account number]

Dear [debtor]:

Here's a reminder that your account of $_____ was overdue as of _____, ____.
Please pay this account promptly. If you have already put the check in the mail, we apologize for the inconvenience and thank you for your payment.

Sincerely,

Collection Letter – Overdue Account (Form 26)

[Debtor's name]
[Street address]
[City, state zip]

[Month day, year]

Re: [account balance]
   [account number]

Dear [debtor]:

This is the second reminder that you owe us $_____. Please pay this account promptly. We would like to continue doing business with you, but we need your cooperation and payment to do so.

Thank you for your prompt attention to this matter.

Sincerely,

Collection Letter – Second Reminder (Form 27)

Customer Management List

Customer ID	Company Name	Contact Name	Billing Address	City	State or Province	Postal Code	Country/Region	Contact Title	Phone Number	Fax Number

Customer Management List (Form 28)

Customer Referral List

Name: _____ Phone: _____

Address: _____

Name: _____ Phone: _____

Address: _____

Name: _____ Phone: _____

Address: _____

Name: _____ Phone: _____

Address: _____

Name: _____ Phone: _____

Address: _____

Name: _____ Phone: _____

Address: _____

Name: _____ Phone: _____

Address: _____

Customer Referral List (Form 29)

Quality Scale Survey

Name: _____

1	Poor
2	Fair
3	Good
4	Very Good
5	Excellent

For each item identified below, circle the number to the right that best fits your judgment of its quality. Use the scale above to select the quality number.

Description / Identification of Survey Item	Scale
1. Insert an Item Description or leave blank	1 2 3 4 5
2. Insert an Item Description or leave blank	1 2 3 4 5
3. Insert an Item Description or leave blank	1 2 3 4 5
4. Insert an Item Description or leave blank	1 2 3 4 5
5. Insert an Item Description or leave blank	1 2 3 4 5
6. Insert an Item Description or leave blank	1 2 3 4 5
7. Insert an Item Description or leave blank	1 2 3 4 5
8. Insert an Item Description or leave blank	1 2 3 4 5
9. Insert an Item Description or leave blank	1 2 3 4 5
10. Insert an Item Description or leave blank	1 2 3 4 5
11. Insert an Item Description or leave blank	1 2 3 4 5
12. Insert an Item Description or leave blank	1 2 3 4 5

Customer Survey – Quality Scale (Form 30)
[Your Name]
[Street Address]
[City, ST ZIP Code]
March 7, 2004

> Customer Survey – Testimonial Form 31

[Recipient Name]
[Title]
[Company Name]
[Street Address]
[City, ST ZIP Code]

Dear [Recipient Name]:

I have a favor to ask of you.

I am in the process of putting together a list of testimonials about my services from satisfied clients like you.

Would you take a few minutes to give me your opinion of my personal organization services? No need to dictate a letter; just jot your comments on the back of this letter, sign below, and return it to me in the enclosed envelope. (The second copy is for your files.)

I look forward to learning what you like about my service…but I welcome any suggestions or criticism.

Many thanks.

Sincerely,

[Your Name]
[Title]

Enclosures

YOU HAVE MY PERMISSION TO QUOTE FROM MY COMMENTS AND USE THESE QUOTATIONS IN ADS, BROCHURES, MAIL, AND OTHER PROMOTIONS USED TO MARKET YOUR PROFESSIONAL ORGANIZING BUSINESS.

Signature _____ Date _____

[Click here and type return address and phone and fax numbers]

Company Name Here

Fax

To:	[Click here and type name]	**From:**	[Click here and type name]
Fax:	[Click here and type fax number]	**Pages:**	[Click here and type # of pages]
Phone:	[Click here and type phone number]	**Date:**	7/5/2004
Re:	[Click here and type subject of fax]	**CC:**	[Click here and type name]

☐ **Urgent** ☐ **For Review** ☐ **Please Comment** ☐ **Please Reply** ☐ **Please Recycle**

- **Comments:** Select this text and delete it or replace it with your own. To save changes to this template for future use, choose Save As from the File menu. In the Save As Type box, choose Document Template. Next time you want to use it, choose New from the File menu, and then double-click your template.

Fax Cover – Professional (Form 32)

© 2006, Lisa Steinbacher, Organize My Life!

[Your Company Name]

[Your Company Slogan]

[Address]
[City, State ZIP Code]
Phone [407.555.0190] Fax [407.555.0191]

INVOICE

INVOICE # [100]
DATE: July 5, 2004

Bill To:
[Name]
[Company]
[Address]
[City, State ZIP Code]
[Phone]

Ship To:
[Name]
[Company]
[Address]
[City, State ZIP Code]
[Phone]

Comments or special instructions:

SALESPERSON	P.O. NUMBER	SHIP DATE	SHIP VIA	F.O.B. POINT	TERMS
					Due on receipt

QUANTITY	DESCRIPTION	UNIT PRICE	AMOUNT
		SUBTOTAL	
		SALES TAX	
		SHIPPING & HANDLING	
		TOTAL DUE	

Make all checks payable to **[Your Company Name]**

Invoice – Product (Form 33)

[Your Company Name]

[Your Company Slogan]

[Address]
[City, ST ZIP Code]
Phone **[303.555.0190]** Fax **[303.555.0191]**

INVOICE

INVOICE # [100]
DATE: July 5, 2004

Bill To:
[Name]
[Company Name]
[Street Address]
[City, ST ZIP Code]
[Phone]

For:
[Project or service description]

DESCRIPTION	AMOUNT
	TOTAL

Make all checks payable to [**Your Company Name**]
If you have any questions concerning this invoice, contact [**Name, Phone Number, E-mail**]

THANK YOU FOR YOUR BUSINESS!

Invoice – Service (Form 34)

[Your Company Name]

[Your Company Slogan]

[Street Address]
[City, ST ZIP Code]
Phone [708.555.0190] Fax [708.555.0191]

INVOICE

DATE: July 5, 2004
INVOICE # [100]

Bill To:
[Name]
[Company Name]
[Street Address]
[City, ST ZIP Code]
[Phone]

For:
[Project or service description]

DESCRIPTION	HOURS	RATE	AMOUNT
			TOTAL

Make all checks payable to [**Your Company Name**]
Total due in 15 days. Overdue accounts subject to a service charge of 1% per month.

THANK YOU FOR YOUR BUSINESS!

Invoice – Time Tracking (Form 35)

JAN 2006	**Item Name Here** • Type Description Here • Type Comments Here	OCT 2006	**Item Name Here** • Type Description Here • Type Comments Here
FEB 2006	**Item Name Here** • Type Description Here • Type Comments Here	NOV 2006	**Item Name Here** • Type Description Here • Type Comments Here
MAR 2006	**Item Name Here** • Type Description Here • Type Comments Here	DEC 2006	**Item Name Here** • Type Description Here • Type Comments Here
APR 2006	**Item Name Here** • Type Description Here • Type Comments Here	JAN 2007	**Item Name Here** • Type Description Here • Type Comments Here
MAY 2006	**Item Name Here** • Type Description Here • Type Comments Here	FEB 2007	**Item Name Here** • Type Description Here • Type Comments Here
JUN 2006	**Item Name Here** • Type Description Here • Type Comments Here	MAR 2007	**Item Name Here** • Type Description Here • Type Comments Here
JU 20	**Item Name Here**	A 20	**Item Name Here**

Label – Date Tab – Multicolor (Form 36)

JAN 2006 — **Item Name Here** • Type Description Here • Type Comments Here	**OCT** 2006 — **Item Name Here** • Type Description Here • Type Comments Here
FEB 2006 — **Item Name Here** • Type Description Here • Type Comments Here	**NOV** 2006 — **Item Name Here** • Type Description Here • Type Comments Here
MAR 2006 — **Item Name Here** • Type Description Here • Type Comments Here	**DEC** 2006 — **Item Name Here** • Type Description Here • Type Comments Here
APR 2006 — **Item Name Here** • Type Description Here • Type Comments Here	**JAN** 2007 — **Item Name Here** • Type Description Here • Type Comments Here
MAY 2006 — **Item Name Here** • Type Description Here • Type Comments Here	**FEB** 2007 — **Item Name Here** • Type Description Here • Type Comments Here
JUN 2006 — **Item Name Here** • Type Description Here • Type Comments Here	**MAR** 2007 — **Item Name Here** • Type Description Here • Type Comments Here
JU 20 — **Item Name Here**	**AP** 20 — **Item Name Here**

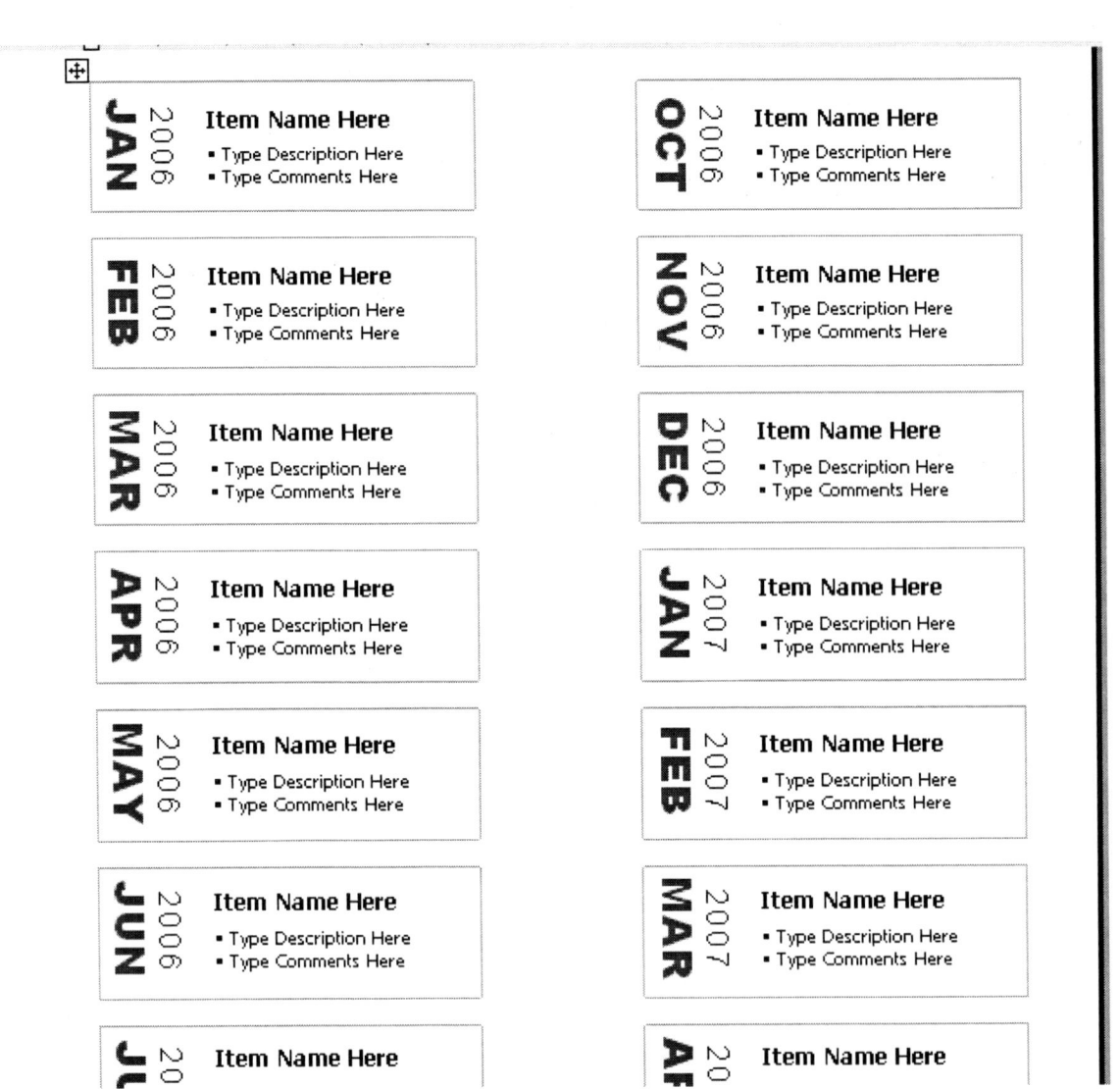

Label – Date Tab – Solid (Form 37)

00000-0000-00	00000-0000-00
Item Name Here • Type Description Here • Type Comments Here	Item Name Here • Type Description Here • Type Comments Here
00000-0000-00	**00000-0000-00**
Item Name Here • Type Description Here • Type Comments Here	Item Name Here • Type Description Here • Type Comments Here
00000-0000-00	**00000-0000-00**
Item Name Here • Type Description Here • Type Comments Here	Item Name Here • Type Description Here • Type Comments Here
00000-0000-00	**00000-0000-00**
Item Name Here • Type Description Here • Type Comments Here	Item Name Here • Type Description Here • Type Comments Here
00000-0000-00	**00000-0000-00**
Item Name Here • Type Description Here • Type Comments Here	Item Name Here • Type Description Here • Type Comments Here
00000-0000-00	**00000-0000-00**
Item Name Here • Type Description Here • Type Comments Here	Item Name Here • Type Description Here • Type Comments Here
00000-0000-00	**00000-0000-00**
Item Name Here • Type Description Here • Type Comments Here	Item Name Here • Type Description Here • Type Comments Here
00000-0000-00	**00000-0000-00**
Item Name Here • Type Description Here • Type Comments Here	Item Name Here • Type Description Here • Type Comments Here

Label - Full Color (Form 38)

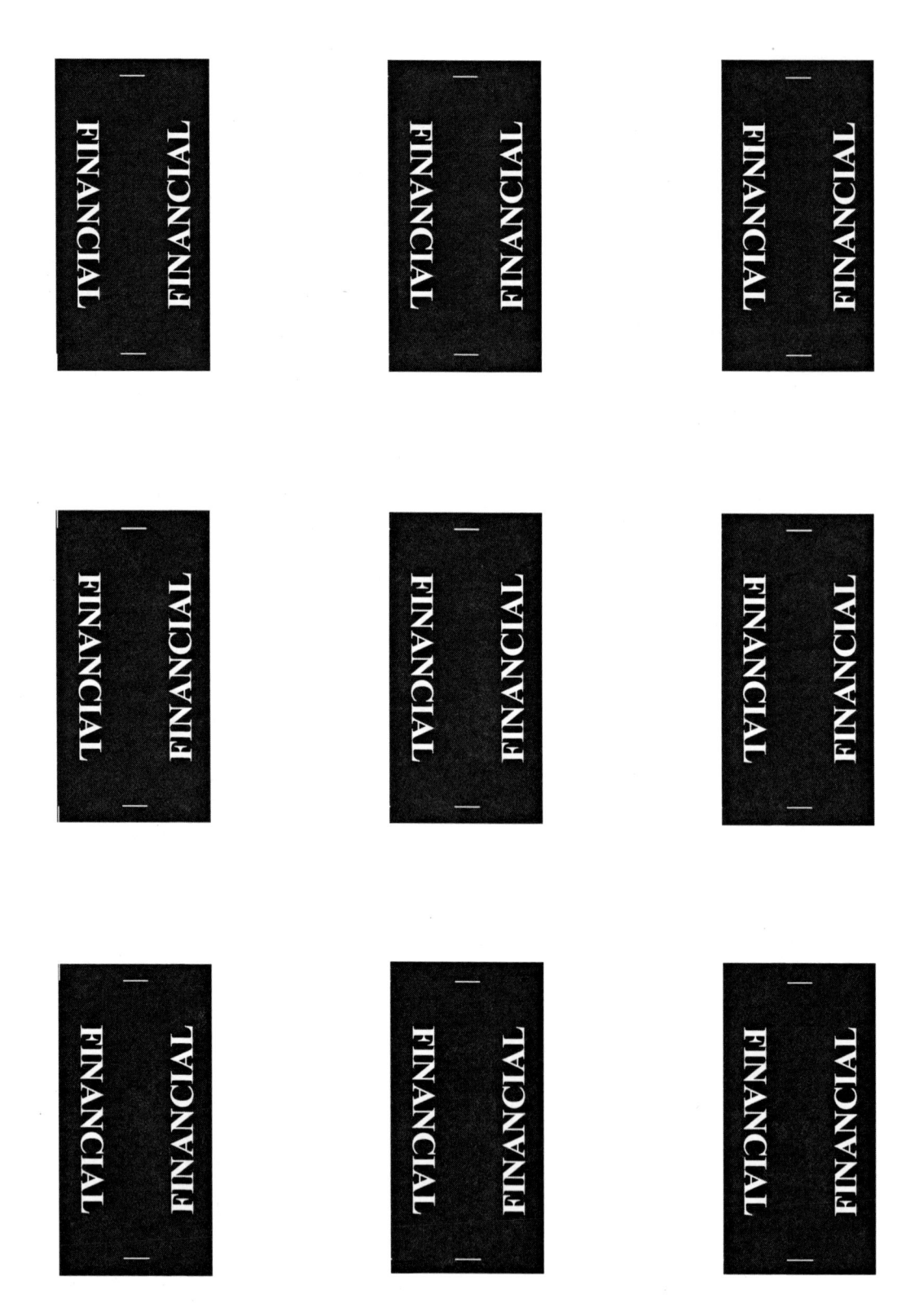

Label – Hanging File Folder (Form 39)

| **Type Name Here**
ID#: 000-0000-00
Dept: Name | **A** | **Type Name Here**
ID#: 000-0000-00
Dept: Name | **J** |
|---|---|---|---|
| **Type Name Here**
ID#: 000-0000-00
Dept: Name | **B** | **Type Name Here**
ID#: 000-0000-00
Dept: Name | **K** |
| **Type Name Here**
ID#: 000-0000-00
Dept: Name | **C** | **Type Name Here**
ID#: 000-0000-00
Dept: Name | **L** |
| **Type Name Here**
ID#: 000-0000-00
Dept: Name | **D** | **Type Name Here**
ID#: 000-0000-00
Dept: Name | **M** |
| **Type Name Here**
ID#: 000-0000-00
Dept: Name | **E** | **Type Name Here**
ID#: 000-0000-00
Dept: Name | **N** |
| **Type Name Here**
ID#: 000-0000-00
Dept: Name | **F** | **Type Name Here**
ID#: 000-0000-00
Dept: Name | **O** |
| **Type Name Here**
ID#: 000-0000-00
Dept: Name | **G** | **Type Name Here**
ID#: 000-0000-00
Dept: Name | **P** |
| **Type Name Here**
ID#: 000-0000-00
Dept: Name | **H** | **Type Name Here**
ID#: 000-0000-00
Dept: Name | **Q** |
| **Type Name Here**
ID#: 000-0000-00
Dept: Name | **I** | **Type Name Here**
ID#: 000-0000-00
Dept: Name | **R** |

Label – Letter Tab – Solid (Form 40)

Project Name
001 – Section Name Here
Dept: Name Here

001

Project Name
002 – Section Name Here
Dept: Name Here

002

Project Name
003 – Section Name Here
Dept: Name Here

003

Project Name
004 – Section Name Here
Dept: Name Here

004

Project Name
005 – Section Name Here
Dept: Name Here

005

Project Name
006 – Section Name Here
Dept: Name Here

006

Project Name
007 – Section Name Here
Dept: Name Here

007

Project Name
008 – Section Name Here
Dept: Name Here

008

Project Name
009 – Section Name Here
Dept: Name Here

009

Project Name
010 – Section Name Here
Dept: Name Here

010

Project Name
011 – Section Name Here
Dept: Name Here

011

Project Name
012 – Section Name Here
Dept: Name Here

012

Project Name
013 – Section Name Here
Dept: Name Here

013

Project Name
014 – Section Name Here
Dept: Name Here

014

Project Name
015 – Section Name Here
Dept: Name Here

015

Project Name
016 – Section Name Here
Dept: Name Here

016

Project Name
017 – Section Name Here
Dept: Name Here

017

Project Name
018 – Section Name Here
Dept: Name Here

018

Label - Project Name (Form 41)

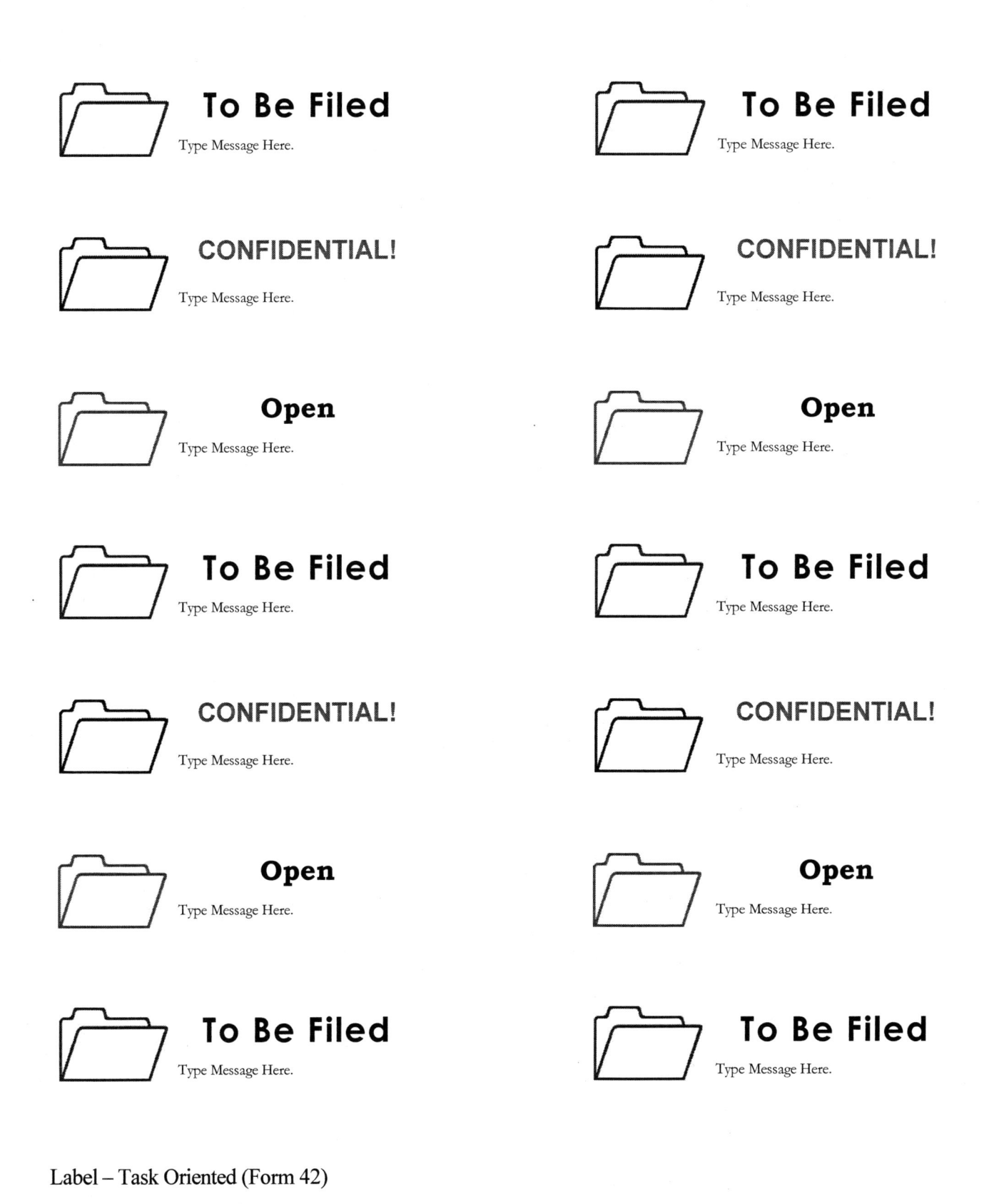

📁	**To Be Filed** Type Message Here.	📁	**To Be Filed** Type Message Here.
📁	**CONFIDENTIAL!** Type Message Here.	📁	**CONFIDENTIAL!** Type Message Here.
📁	**Open** Type Message Here.	📁	**Open** Type Message Here.
📁	**To Be Filed** Type Message Here.	📁	**To Be Filed** Type Message Here.
📁	**CONFIDENTIAL!** Type Message Here.	📁	**CONFIDENTIAL!** Type Message Here.
📁	**Open** Type Message Here.	📁	**Open** Type Message Here.
📁	**To Be Filed** Type Message Here.	📁	**To Be Filed** Type Message Here.

Label – Task Oriented (Form 42)

Goals	Resume Samples
Current Resume	Advertisements
Job Descriptions	Target Companies
Benefit Expectations	Comparable Salary
Avery Dennison Research	Microsoft Research
BRR Technologies Research	MLH Systems Research
Cover Letters	Follow Up Correspondence
Interview Questions	Portfolio
Plan & Schedule	Motivational Information
January	February
March	April
May	June

Label – Text – White (Form 43)

Assessment Form

Name: _____ **Date of Assessment:** _____

Location of Project:
☐ Residence   ☐ Business (List industry: _____)

Specific Area of Concentration:

☐	Kitchen	☐	Living Room	☐	Dining Room	☐	Den/Office
☐	Bedroom 1	☐	Bedroom 2	☐	Bedroom 3	☐	Bedroom 4
☐	Bathroom 1	☐	Bathroom 2	☐	Bathroom 3	☐	Garage
☐	Storage	☐	Basement	☐	Play Area	☐	Supply Closet
☐	Filing Area	☐	Family Room	☐		☐	
☐		☐		☐		☐	

Specific Problem:

☐	Clutter Control	☐	Filing System	☐	Paper Flow	☐	Storage
☐	Reorganization	☐	Time Mgmnt	☐	Priority	☐	Planning
☐	Delegation	☐	Records Mgmnt	☐	Bills/Finances	☐	Pack Rat
☐		☐		☐		☐	
☐		☐		☐		☐	

List Detailed Problems Areas:

1.
2.
3.
4.
5.
6.

Recommended Solution:

☐	Reorganization	☐	Products	☐	General Consult	☐	Referral
☐		☐		☐		☐	

List Detailed Recommended Solutions:

1.
2.
3.
4.
5.
6.

Other Information:

Needs Assessment (Form 44)

TREY RESEARCH

12345 Main Street
Anacortes, WA 22305
Phone 323-555-0190
Fax 323-555-0191

Press Release

Contact: Derik Stenerson
Phone: (323) 555-0190

FOR IMMEDIATE RELEASE
9 AM EDT, September 23, 2003

HOW TO CUSTOMIZE THIS PRESS RELEASE

TO OPTIMIZE THE GRAY SHADING for your printer, click on the text area, and choose Borders and Shading from the Format menu. Select a new shade or pattern, and choose OK.

TO CUSTOMIZE THIS TEMPLATE:
Insert your company information in place of the sample text, and change the header on page 2 (for multi-page stories).
Choose File Save As. Choose Document Template in the Save File as Type: box.
To create a new document, choose File New to re-open your customized template as a document.

TO DELETE A TEXTBOX, click on the border (the handles should become highlighted), and press Delete.

-End-

News Release – Elegant (Form 45)

Contact: Sue Smith
My Own Company
Phone 676 555 0190
Fax 676 555 0191

12345 Main Street
Portland, OR 32345
Phone 676 555 0190
Fax 676 555 0191

My Own Company!

Press Release

My Own Company Offers Businesses Real Solutions.

Serves up big ideas for organizing and time management solutions for large and small companies.

Portland, OR, September 23, 2003: When writing a press release, say *who*, *what*, *when*, *where* and *why* in the first paragraph, if you can. Study your newspaper and notice how deftly most writers work that type of information into the first paragraph of each article. In addition, it is helpful if you remember the following:

- Know your contact's name, title, telephone, fax and department.
- Mail or fax your release 10 days in advance of the release date. If there is no specific release date, in the footer of this document, remove the release date, insert the words "For Immediate Release. No Kill Date." This tells the editor that they can use the story whenever they need a "filler" or whenever they have available space.

How to Customize This Press Release

To create your own customized version of this template:

1. Insert your company information in the company name, contact, address and release date frames, and change the header text on page 2 to reflect the contents of your story.
2. Choose File Save As. At the bottom of the menu, choose Document Template in the Save File as Type: box (the filename extensions should change from *.doc* to *.dot*).
3. To create a document, choose File New to re-open your template as a document.

-END-

For Release 9 a.m. EDT, September 23, 1998

News Release – Professional (Form 46)

NEWS RELEASE

Attention: _____ (Editor)
Contact: _____ (You)
Business: _____
Address: _____
City/State/Zip: _____
Phone: _____
Fax/Email: _____
Website: _____

FOR IMMEDIATE RELEASE
NO KILL DATE (date offer ends)
(or)
KILL
DATE:_____

Title:_____

CITY, STATE – First paragraph. State who, what, when, where and why all within the first paragraph.

_____
_____
_____
_____
_____

Second paragraph. State how readers can get your product or offer. Give them more than one method of response. If necessary, include more details on information given in the first paragraph.

_____
_____
_____
_____
_____

Conclusion. State website address where they can get more information.

_____
_____
_____
_____

-END-

Page 1 of 1

News Release Worksheet (Form 47)

Type the Title here

Newsletter Date
Volume 1, Issue 1

Company Name (503)555-0167

YOUR LOGO HERE

Special Interest Articles:

- Add or highlight your point of interest here.
- Add or highlight your point of interest here.
- Add or highlight your point of interest here.

Individual Highlights:

Inside Story	2
Inside Story	3
Inside Story	4
Inside Story	5
Inside Story	6
Inside Story	7
Last Story	8

Lead Story Headline

The purpose of a newsletter is to provide specialized information to a targeted audience. Newsletters can be a great way to market your product or service, and also to create credibility and build your organization's identity among peers, members, employees, or vendors.

First, determine the audience of the newsletter. This could be anyone who might benefit from the information it contains, for example, employees or people interested in purchasing a product or in requesting your services.

You can compile a mailing list from business reply cards, customer information sheets, business cards collected at trade shows, or membership lists. You might consider purchasing a mailing list from a company.

Next, establish how much time and money you can spend on your newsletter. These factors will help determine how frequently you publish the newsletter and its length.

Second Story Headline

The purpose of a newsletter is to provide specialized information to a targeted audience. Newsletters can be a great way to market your product or service, and also to create credibility and build your organization's identity among peers, members, employees, or vendors.

First, determine the audience of the newsletter. This could be anyone who might benefit from the information it contains, for example, employees or people interested in purchasing a product or in requesting your services.

You can compile a mailing list from business reply cards, customer information sheets, business cards collected at trade shows, or membership lists. You might consider purchasing a mailing list from a company.

Next, establish how much time and money you can spend on your newsletter. These factors will help determine how frequently you publish the newsletter and its length.

Newsletter – Aztec (Form 48)

E-Mail Newsletter

<<Add Date>> Volume 1, Number 1

"Make sure you don't lose the customers you've spent so much energy to acquire."

Keep these things in mind for a newsletter with impact:

- Use big headlines.
- Make your articles short and to the point.
- All information should be of value to the customer.

Staying in Touch with Customers

Often businesses spend as much time and effort gathering new customers as they do on anything else. It's also one of the most costly functions of doing business. So it's important to make sure you don't lose the customers you've spent so much energy to acquire. The alternative is to continue with the time-consuming process of finding new customers from an ever shrinking pool of prospects. And since it costs much less to keep existing customers instead of constantly replacing them, it just makes good business sense to do what it takes to keep them coming back.

Regular communication with your customers lets them know how much you value them and their business. Show them you care by offering valuable information such as tips on how to utilize your products and services more effectively, event announcements, information on upcoming new products and expanded services, and special discounts on existing ones.

E-Mail Newsletters—Quick, Easy

Utilizing an e-mail newsletter can be an effective, low-cost method for staying in touch with your customers. It helps reduce churn and can easily generate more business from customers you've already spent a great deal of effort to win. Since there are no mailing and printing costs involved, it's also very gentle to your bottom-line. Another benefit is the almost instantaneous delivery e-mail affords you. You don't have to worry whether the post office will get the newsletter to your customers in time for them to take advantage of a special offer.

Microsoft Office makes it simple to create and send a powerful e-mail newsletter for maximum impact. Customers will appreciate the regular communication and you'll be rewarded with more business from your existing customer base.

Create a Customized Template

Add your company logo, change the colors to reflect the ones your business uses, put in your business address, phone numbers, Web site address—in other words develop a basic template reflecting your company's look that will stay the same for each issue.

It's a good idea to use the Web Layout view (**View\Web Layout**) when creating your newsletter. That's the look your customers will be seeing when they receive your e-mail.

Newsletter – Email (Form 49)

Newsletter Date
Volume 1, Issue 1

Newsletter Title

Company Name (111) 111-1111

Special Interest Articles:

- Add a highlight or your point of interest here.
- Add a highlight or your point of interest here.
- Add a highlight or your point of interest here.

Individual Highlights:

Inside Story	2
Inside Story	3
Inside Story	4
Inside Story	5
Last Story	6

Lead Story Headline

The purpose of a newsletter is to provide specialized information to a targeted audience. Newsletters can be a great way to market your product or service, and also create credibility and build your organization's identity among peers, members, employees, or vendors.

First, determine the audience of the newsletter. This could be anyone who might benefit from the information it contains, for example, employees or people interested in purchasing a product or requesting your service.

You can compile a mailing list from business reply cards, customer information sheets, Business cards collected at trade shows, or membership lists. You might consider purchasing a mailing list from a company.

If you explore the Project Gallery, you will find many publications that match the style of your newsletter.

Next, establish how much time and money you can spend on your newsletter. These factors will help determine how frequently you publish the newsletter and its length.

Second Story Headline

The purpose of a newsletter is to provide specialized information to a targeted audience. Newsletters can be a great way to market your product or service, and also create credibility and build your organization's identity among peers, members, employees, or vendors.

First, determine the audience of the newsletter. This could be anyone who might benefit from the information it contains, for example, employees or people interested in purchasing a product or requesting your service.

You can compile a mailing list from business reply cards, customer information sheets, Business cards collected at trade shows, or membership lists. You might consider purchasing a mailing list from a company.

If you explore the Project Gallery, you will find many publications that match the style of your newsletter.

Next, establish how much time and money you can spend on your newsletter. These factors will help determine how frequently you publish the newsletter and its length. It's recommended that you publish your newsletter at least quarterly so that it's considered a consistent source of information. Your customers or employees will look forward to its arrival.

Newsletter – Professional (Form 50)

PARTNERSHIP AGREEMENT

Partnership agreement made on _____ [date], between _____ [A.B.], of _____ [address], _____ [city], _____ County, _____ [state], and _____ [C.D.], of _____ [address], _____ [city], _____ County, _____ [state] ("partners").

RECITALS

A. Partners desire to join together for the pursuit of common business goals.

B. Partners have considered various forms of joint business enterprises for their business activities.

C. Partners desire to enter into a partnership agreement as the most advantageous business form for their mutual purposes.

In consideration of the mutual promises contained in this agreement, partners agree as follows:

ARTICLE ONE

NAME, PURPOSE, AND DOMICILE

The name of the partnership shall be _____. The partnership shall be conducted for the purposes of _____. The principal place of business shall be at _____ [address], _____ [city], _____ County, _____ [state], unless relocated by majority consent of the partners.

ARTICLE TWO

DURATION OF AGREEMENT

The term of this agreement shall be for _____ years, commencing on _____ [date], and terminating on _____ [date], unless sooner terminated by mutual consent of the parties or by operation of the provisions of this

Partnership Agreement (Form 51)
(Note entire document is seven pages.)

To: **[Recipient Name]**

From: **[Your Name]**

Date: April 9, 2004

Re: **[Subject]**

Thanks for taking the time to chat with me. Here is the memo I promised to fax today. Questions? Call me at (423) 555-0191.

I. OVERVIEW

Contoso, Ltd. markets credit card enhancement programs to banks, department stores, and oil companies.

Sales have been primarily via telemarketing. Contoso, Ltd. is looking to develop profitable direct mail packages as an alternative. The objective is to bring in new members at a cost per order of $40 to $43.

II. CONCEPTS AND METHODOLOGY

Here are the steps normally involved in having me write a package for you:

- Research
- Presentation of concepts (package outline)
- First draft of copy
- Revisions

III. ASSIGNMENT

As discussed, my first choice would be to work on travel arrangements. I've done a lot of work in the travel industry, and wrote a package offering a similar set of enhanced benefits to magazine subscribers.

My second choice is health trends. With changes in health care today, people are uncertain about the status of their coverage. Again, almost everyone is going to use the service at least once or twice, so it will pay back its cost.

IV. TIMING

If you can turn around copy reviews within a week or so, it's realistic for us to have final approved copy in November, in time to make a January mailing.

Proposal – Outline Format (Form 52)

Organize My Life!

Project Proposal Terms and Conditions

In consideration of the services described in this proposal by _____, I acknowledge, understand and agree to the following terms and conditions:

Payment:

- Client(s) initial paid deposit will be subtracted from the final cost. A pro rata portion of the balance will be required at the end of each session as described below:

  Session 1:
  Session 2:
  Session 3:

- Payment should be made payable to "_____" and may be made by check, money order, or cash. There will be a charge of $35 for any checks returned for insufficient funds or any bank draft items that are not payable for any reason, as well as additional collection and/or legal fees up to 40% of original project cost in order to compensate for overdraft charges and unpaid account balances. In the event that a Client(s) is unable to pay the initial deposit, it may be waived at the discretion of the _____ proprietor, and alternate payment arrangements made, which shall be placed in writing and signed by both proprietor and Client(s).

- Client(s) is responsible for paying for agreed-upon supplies (file folders, labels, storage containers, racks, etc.) necessary for the completion of this project. _____ will assist Client(s) either by assisting in shopping for the supplies, or in purchasing the supplies for the Client(s). If _____ purchases supplies on behalf of the Client(s), all supplies will be listed on a Purchase Order form and the Client(s) must sign agreeing to pay the stated amount on the purchase order prior to delivery of the supplies. All supplies must be ordered and delivered to Client(s) home or office prior to the first session date.

- Client(s) is responsible for any travel fees detailed on the reverse of this proposal. Travel fees shall only be incurred if Client(s) is located more than 30 minutes away from _____. If travel fees are not listed, none will be incurred.

Schedules/Cancellation Fee:

- Schedules shall be set by verbal mutual agreement between Client(s) and _____ Professional Organizer(s) at the time of proposal agreement or anytime thereafter.

- Cancellation of a scheduled appointment must be done within 24 hours prior to the date scheduled. Failure to keep any appointment without prior notification OR failure to cancel an appointment within 24 hours prior to the appointment time will be considered a "No Show / Late Cancel" and a fee of $50.00 will be charged; under extenuating emergency circumstances determined by proprietor, this fee may be waived.

- Client(s) is required to be present during organizing sessions and to assist with the projects. It is very important that Client(s) and professional organizer(s) can focus on the session. Therefore, Client(s) must make arrangements for handling incoming phone calls, redirecting visitors, childcare etc. so that sessions are not interrupted.

Performance/Delivery Guarantee:

- _____ agrees to fulfill the proposed solutions within the amount of time indicated in this proposal, for the proposed price indicated. If _____ underestimates the time it takes to do the written proposed project, another session will be added to complete the project. Should this occur, the Client(s) will not be charged more than the original proposed amount.

- _____ strives to meet a 100% Client(s) satisfaction level. If we failed to meet any of the proposed solutions as detailed in this proposal, provide us within seven business days, a written letter describing what work or parts of the project were not met. Letter should be mailed via return receipt to: _____. _____ will then schedule a complimentary session to make necessary adjustments. Failure to make a claim within seven business days implies that you fully accept the completed work at the agreed-upon price.

Proposal – Terms and Conditions (Form 53)

Proposal Worksheet

Name:_____ **Date:**_____

Detailed Problem Areas:

1.
2.
3.
4.
5.
6.

Detailed Recommended Solutions:

1.
2.
3.
4.
5.
6.

Recommended Products:

1.
2.
3.
4.
5.
6.

Complimentary Additions:

Proposal Worksheet (Form 54)

© 2006, Lisa Steinbacher, Organize My Life!

Prospect Data Sheet

First Contact

Name	
Company	
Address	
Home Phone	Secondary Phone
Email	
Initial Contact Date	
Date Offer Sent	

Follow Up Contacts

Date	Next Follow Up Date
Contact Method	☐ Phone ☐ Mail ☐ Email ☐ Visit ☐ NO CONTACT ACHIEVED
Result	☐ Initial Consultation ☐ Set Appointment ☐ Not Interested Now ☐ End Contact Effort
Interest Level	☐ One ☐ Two ☐ Three ☐ Four ☐ Five (1 lowest - 5 highest)
Notes	

Date	Next Follow Up Date
Contact Method	☐ Phone ☐ Mail ☐ Email ☐ Visit ☐ NO CONTACT ACHIEVED
Result	☐ Initial Consultation ☐ Set Appointment ☐ Not Interested Now ☐ End Contact Effort
Interest Level	☐ One ☐ Two ☐ Three ☐ Four ☐ Five (1 lowest - 5 highest)
Notes	

Date	Next Follow Up Date
Contact Method	☐ Phone ☐ Mail ☐ Email ☐ Visit ☐ NO CONTACT ACHIEVED
Result	☐ Initial Consultation ☐ Set Appointment ☐ Not Interested Now ☐ End Contact Effort
Interest Level	☐ One ☐ Two ☐ Three ☐ Four ☐ Five (1 lowest - 5 highest)
Notes	

Date	Next Follow Up Date
Contact Method	☐ Phone ☐ Mail ☐ Email ☐ Visit ☐ NO CONTACT ACHIEVED
Result	☐ Initial Consultation ☐ Set Appointment ☐ Not Interested Now ☐ End Contact Effort
Interest Level	☐ One ☐ Two ☐ Three ☐ Four ☐ Five (1 lowest - 5 highest)
Notes	

Prospect Data Sheet (Form 55)

[Your Company Name]
[Your Company Slogan]

[Street Address]
[City, ST ZIP Code]
Phone [509.555.0190] Fax [509.555.0191]

PURCHASE ORDER

The following number must appear on all related correspondence, shipping papers, and invoices:

P.O. NUMBER: [100]

To:
[Name]
[Company Name]
[Street Address]
[City, ST ZIP Code]
[Phone]

Ship To:
[Name]
[Company Name]
[Street Address]
[City, ST ZIP Code]
[Phone]

P.O. DATE	REQUISITIONER	SHIPPED VIA	F.O.B. POINT	TERMS

QTY	UNIT	DESCRIPTION	UNIT PRICE	TOTAL

SUBTOTAL	
SALES TAX	
SHIPPING & HANDLING	
OTHER	
TOTAL	

1. Please send two copies of your invoice.
2. Enter this order in accordance with the prices, terms, delivery method, and specifications listed above.
3. Please notify us immediately if you are unable to ship as specified.
4. **Send all correspondence to:**
   [Name]
   [Street Address]
   [City, ST ZIP Code]
   Phone [509.555.0190] Fax [509.555.0191]

_____   _____
Authorized by   Date

Purchase Order (Form 56)

© 2006, Lisa Steinbacher, Organize My Life!

	Receipt	No.	
Payee Name: Address: City, State ZIP:		Payer Name: Address: City, State ZIP:	
Date	**Description**		**Amount**
		Subtotal	
		Tax	
Total			

	Receipt	No.	
Payee Name: Address: City, State ZIP:		Payer Name: Address: City, State ZIP:	
Date	**Description**		**Amount**
		Subtotal	
		Tax	
Total			

	Receipt	No.	
Payee Name: Address: City, State ZIP:		Payer Name: Address: City, State ZIP:	
Date	**Description**		**Amount**
		Subtotal	
		Tax	
Total			

Receipts (Form 57)

[Your Name]
[Street Address]
[City, ST ZIP Code]
April 9, 2004

[Recipient Name]
[Title]
[Company Name]
[Street Address]
[City, ST ZIP Code]

Dear [Recipient Name]:

I have a favor to ask of you.

I am in the process of putting together a list of testimonials about my services from satisfied clients like you.

Would you take a few minutes to give me your opinion of my organizing services? No need to dictate a letter; just jot your comments on the back of this letter, sign below, and return it to me in the enclosed envelope. (The second copy is for your files.)

I look forward to learning what you like about my service…but I welcome any suggestions or criticism.

Many thanks.

Sincerely,

[Your Name]
[Title]

Enclosures

YOU HAVE MY PERMISSION TO QUOTE FROM MY COMMENTS AND USE THESE QUOTATIONS IN ADS, BROCHURES, MAIL, AND OTHER PROMOTIONS USED TO MARKET YOUR PROFESSIONAL ORGANIZING SERVICES.

Signature _____ Date _____

Testimonial – Request To Write (Form 58)

[Your Name]
[Street Address]
[City, ST ZIP Code]
April 9, 2004

[Recipient Name]
[Title]
[Company Name]
[Street Address]
[City, ST ZIP Code]

Dear [Recipient Name]:

Thank you so much for your letter of May 15 (copy attached). It is always nice to hear when things are going right!

You have said such positive things about us that I would like to quote from this letter in the ads, brochures, direct mail packages, and other promotions that I use to market my business - with your permission, of course. If this is okay with you, would you please sign the bottom of this letter and send it back to me in the enclosed envelope? (The second copy is for your files.) Thank you once again!

Sincerely,

[Your Name]
[Title]

Enclosure

YOU HAVE MY PERMISSION TO QUOTE FROM THE ATTACHED LETTER IN ADS, BROCHURES, MAIL, AND OTHER PROMOTIONS USED TO MARKET YOUR PROFESSIONAL ORGANIZING SERVICES.

Signature _____ Date _____

Testimonial – Request To Use (Form 59)

Appendix B: Contact Management Database Instructions

Below are the instructions for using the Contact Management Database:

Select the "Databases" folder from the group of icons on your Forms CD or in the Forms Folder from the downloaded version of the book.

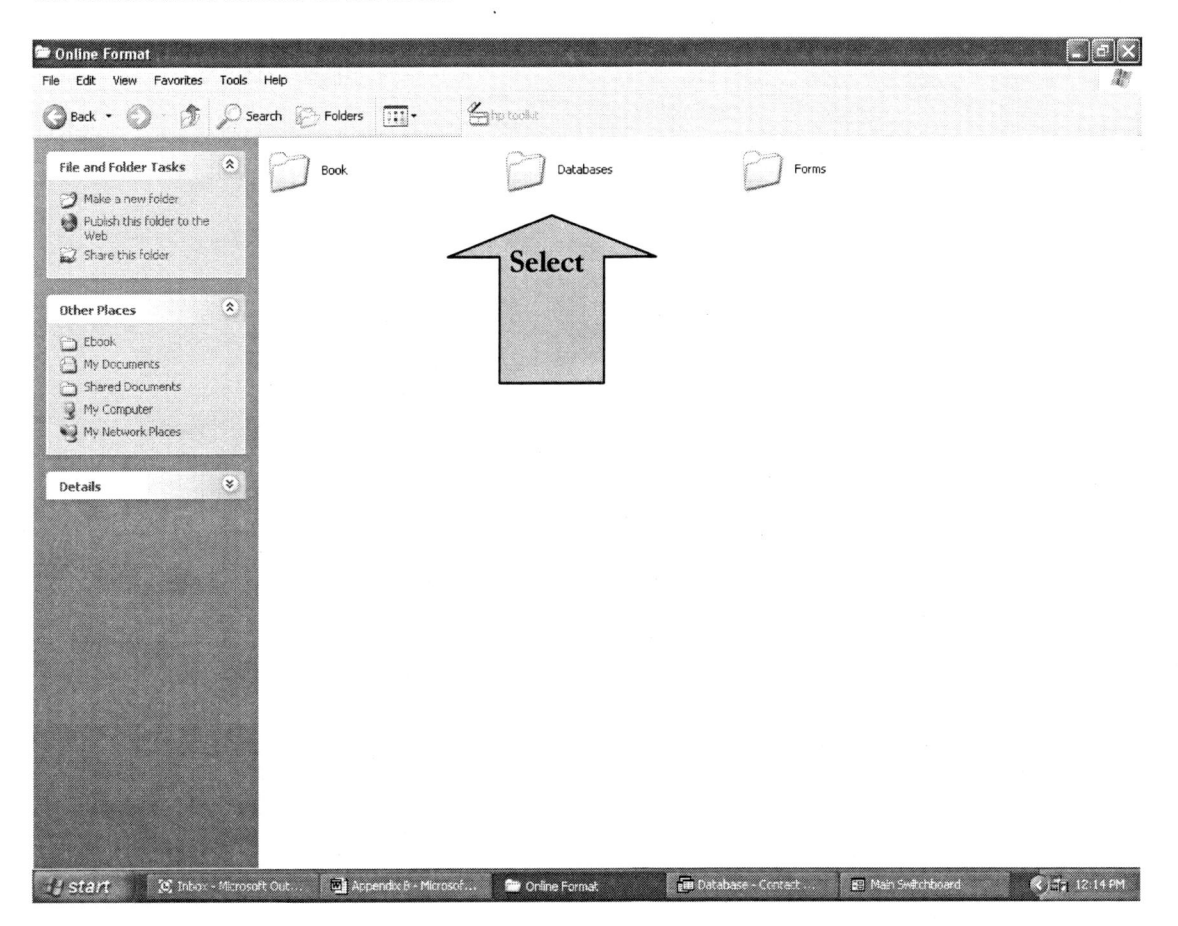

Select the "Database – Contact Management" icon from the list in the Databases directory. The accompanying icon will be a piece of paper with a red key inside a box.

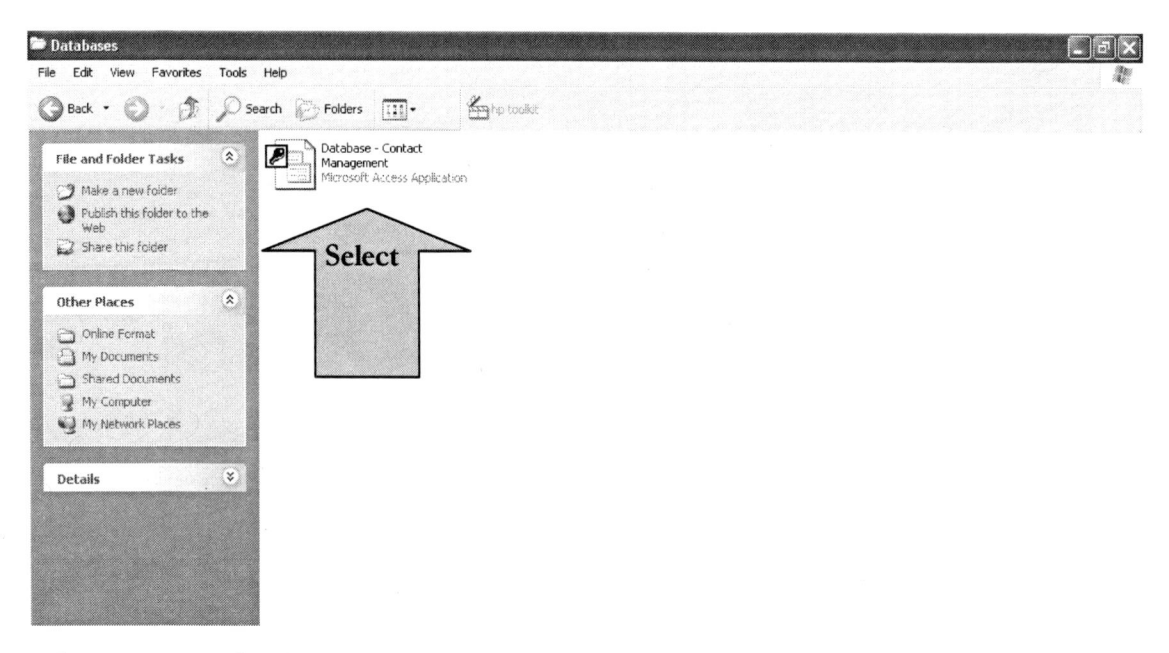

When you open the Contact Management Database, the screen shown below will appear. This screen allows you multiple options. The first option is "Enter/View Contacts", which will take you to a new screen where you can enter contact information and view current contact entries. The next option is "Preview Reports…". This will take you to a secondary screen where you can select the type of report to view and if desired, print them. The last option is "Exit this database" which will exit the database.

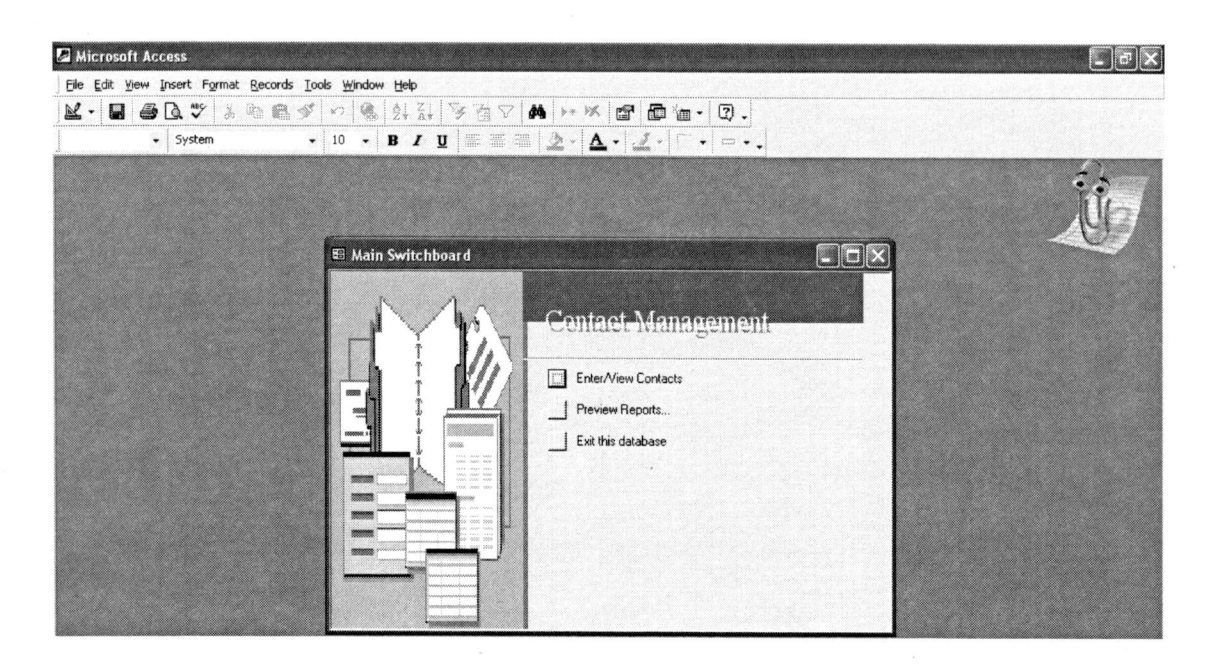

Click "Enter/View Contacts".

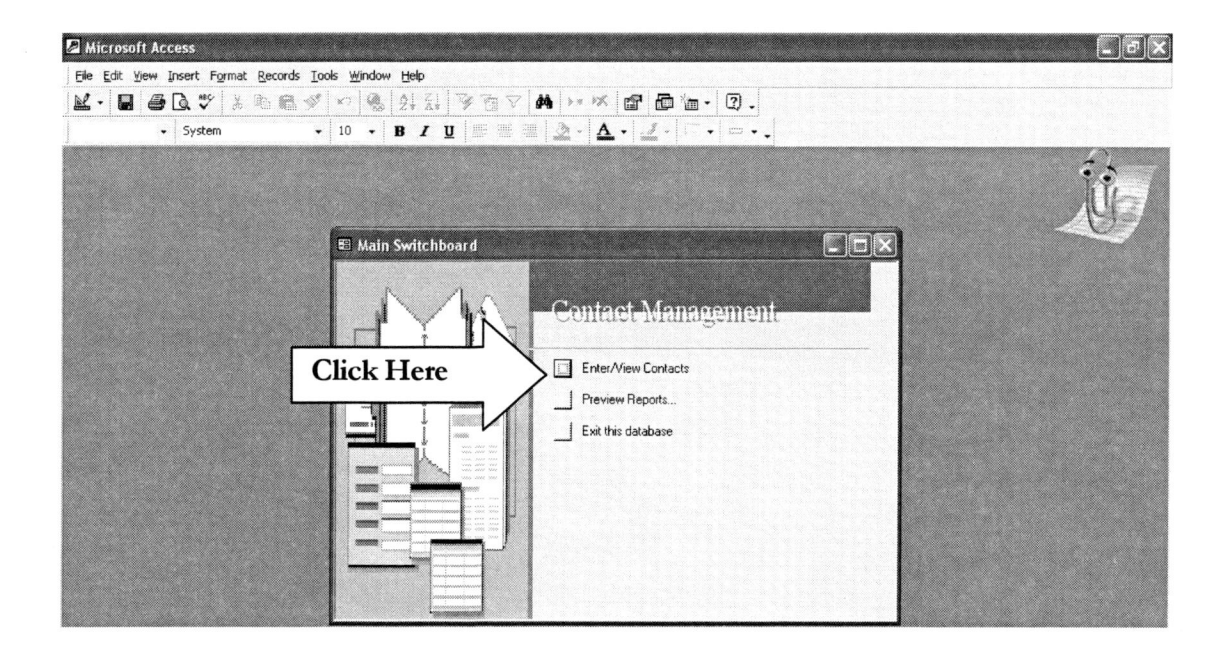

A new window appears. This is the contact entry window. From here, you can enter the information in each field as needed. (The first record is a sample that can be deleted if desired.) Note that the "Dear" field is where you enter the salutation for your contact; if you ever create a letter from this database, you may want the letter to address the contact as "Dear Jane" or "Dear Ms. Smith". In this case, you would type the name "Jane" in the box, or "Ms. Smith". When you complete the information for this screen, click the button on the bottom center that is the number "2".

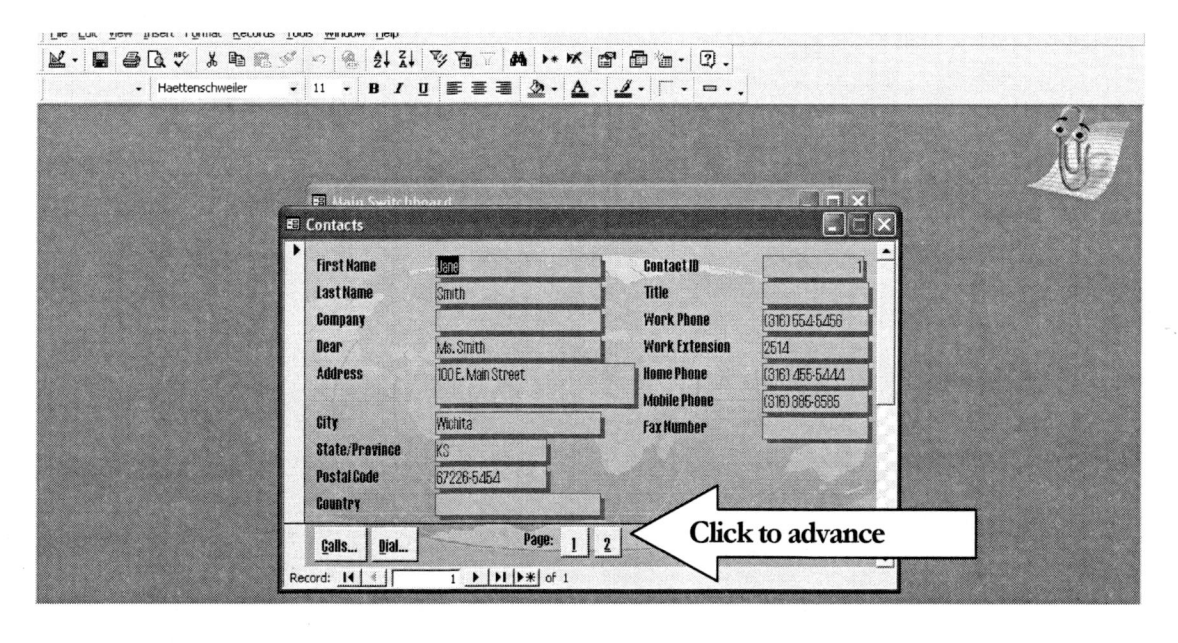

The second entry screen is shown below. In the field "Contact Type", click the down arrow, and you will see three options to choose from: Cold Call, Customer, and Prospect. In Chapter 4 of the book, I covered the difference between these three contact categories. Select the most appropriate option for your contact, and update it as necessary when your customer moves from one category to another. The "Referred By" field is great for tracking how customers heard about your business, so you can see how your marketing campaigns are doing. The "Notes" field is a great place to write any note about the customer's needs or preferences. If you call the customer, you can easily track the call by clicking the "Calls" button on the bottom left of the entry screen.

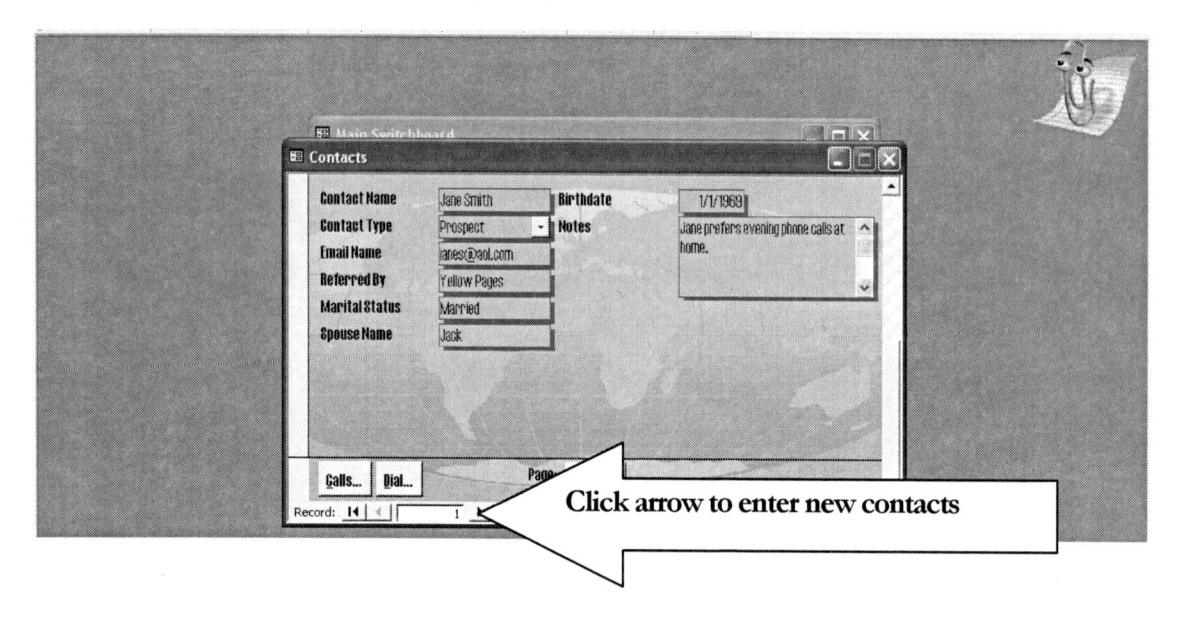

Click arrow to enter new contacts

If you click your mouse on the "Calls" button on the bottom left of the screen, the window shown below will appear. The database automatically enters the date and time, and allows you to enter a subject (such as "follow up call #1") and has a large space for call notes on the bottom. To close the window, click the small red "X" in the top right corner of the window.

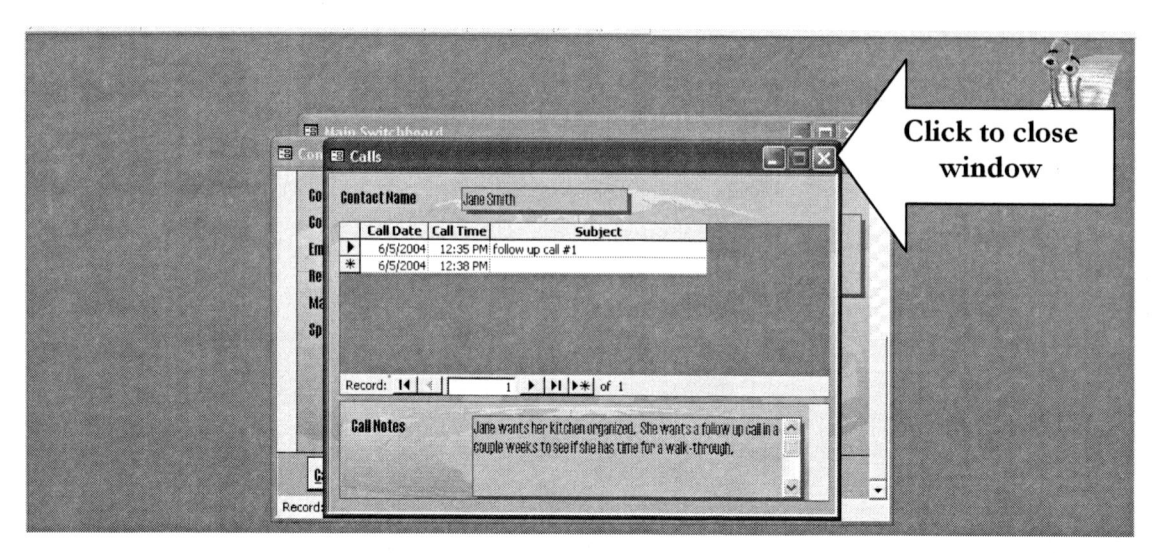

Click to close window

After you click the red "X" in the corner of the "Calls" window, you will be taken back to the "Contacts" window. Click the red "X" in this window to close it and take you back to the "Main Switchboard".

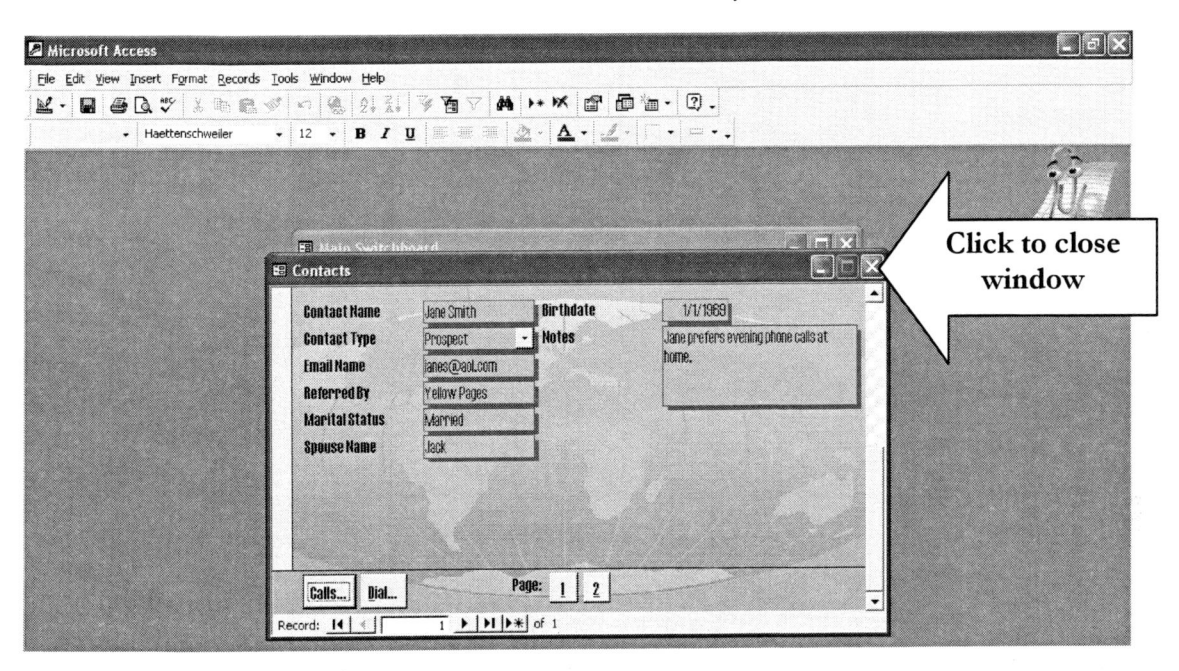

We will look at the reports next. To view reports, at the main switchboard window, click "Preview Reports".

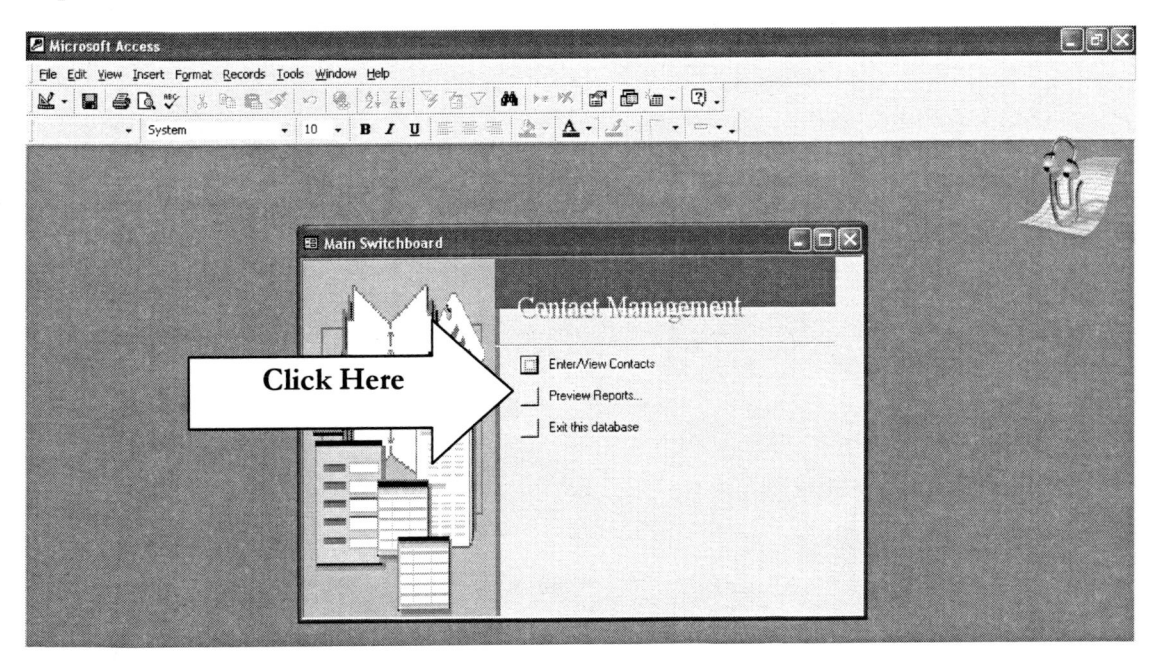

A new submenu will appear (next picture).

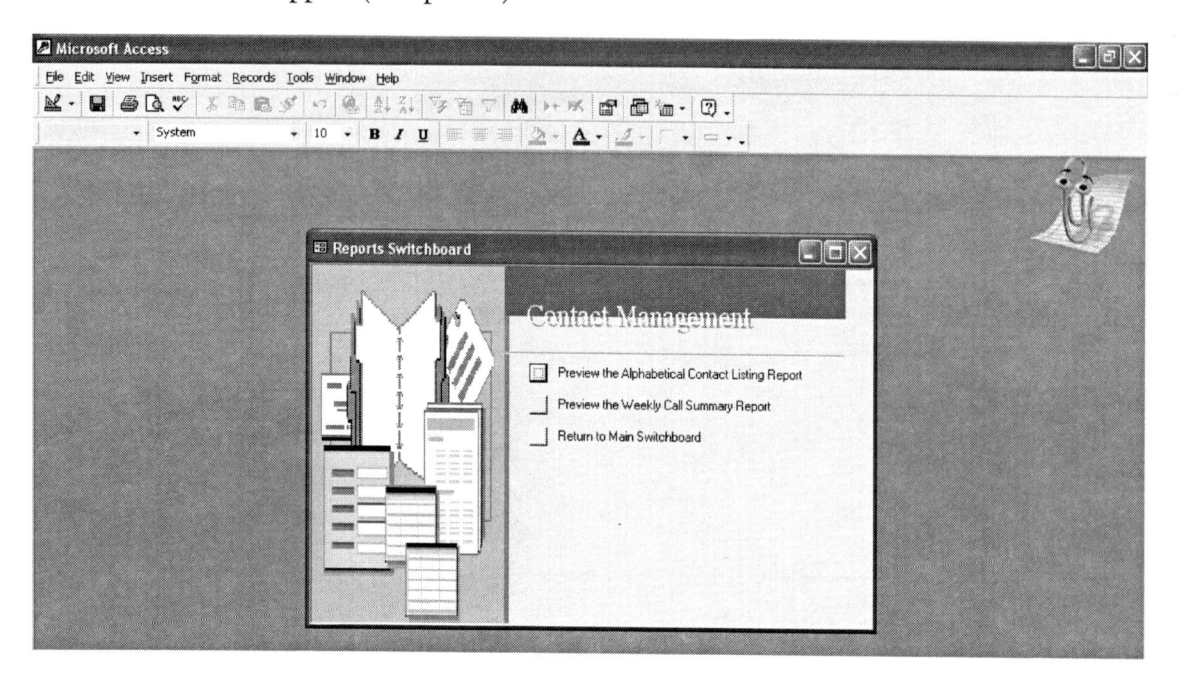

This allows you to select the specific report you would like to view. There are two preformatted reports. The first, "Alphabetical Contact Listing" is an alphabetical list of all your contacts. The second, "Weekly Call Summary" is a call report where you can select customized dates to view call records. If you click the second report "Weekly Call Summary", a submenu will display. Enter the beginning date and the ending date you want to view, and then click "Preview" to view the report (shown below).

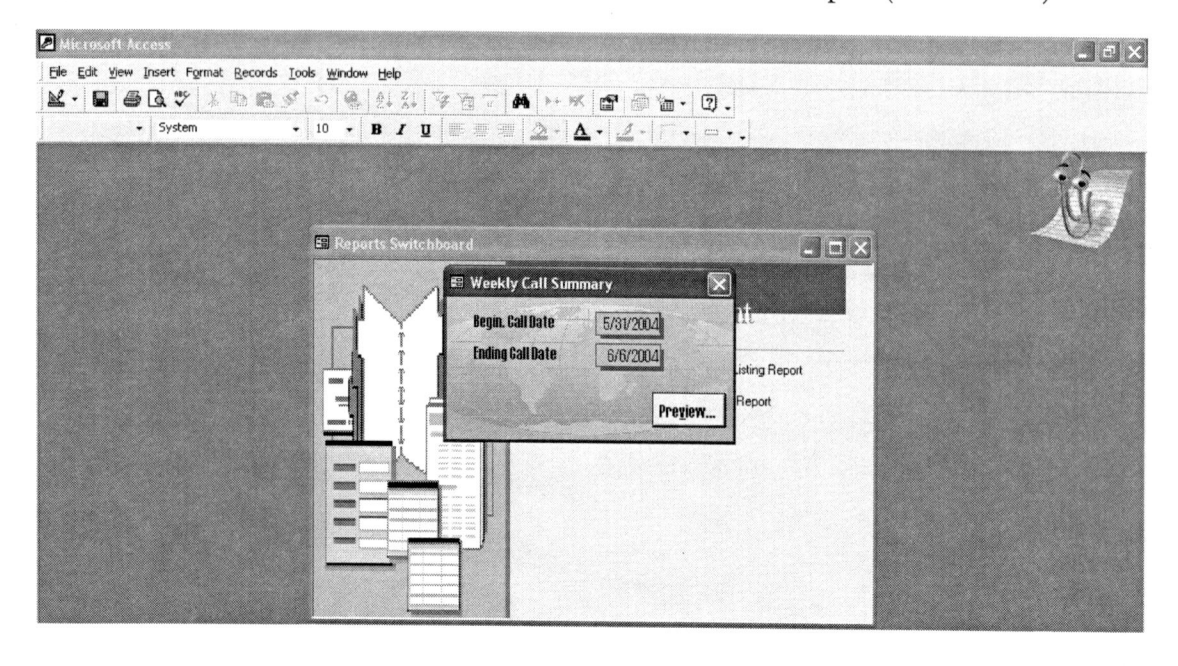

The next two images below are sample screens of the Weekly Call Summary and the Alphabetical Contact Listing report. To close any report, click the red "X" in the upper right corner of the report window.

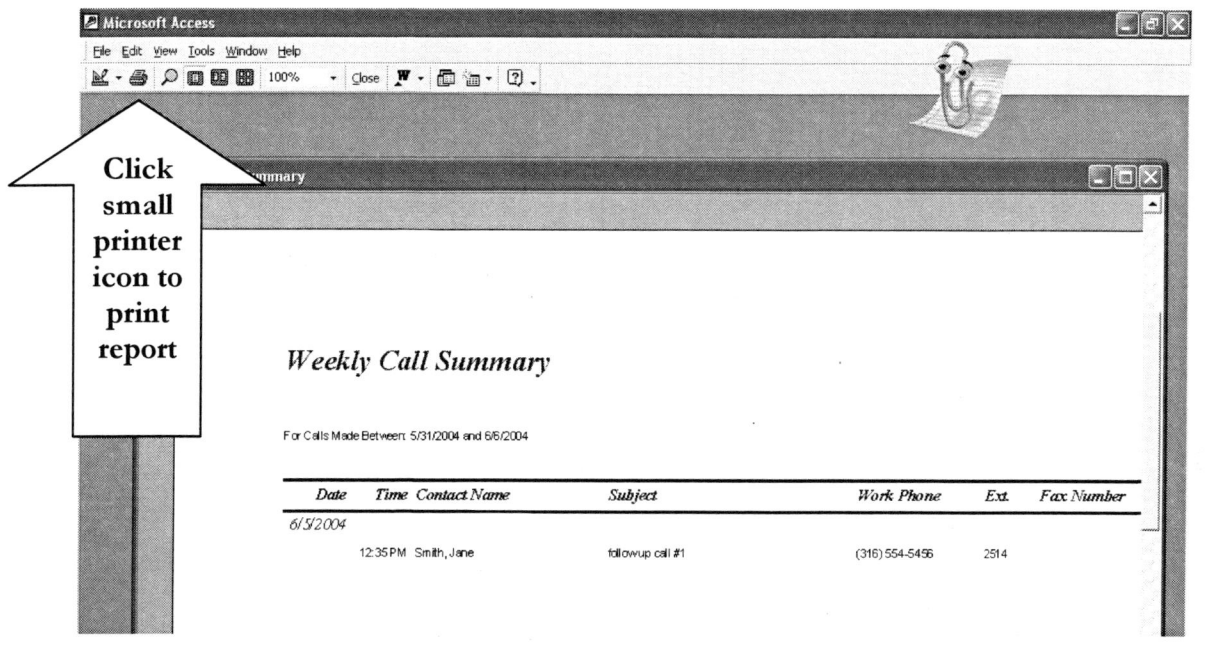

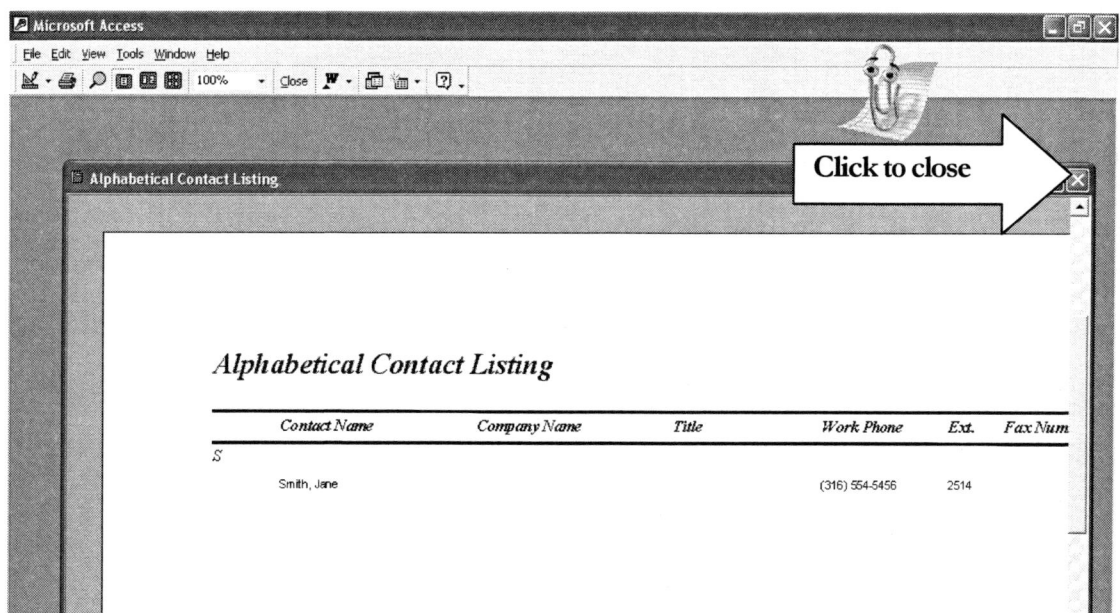

Click small printer icon to print report

Weekly Call Summary

For Calls Made Between: 5/31/2004 and 6/6/2004

Date	Time	Contact Name	Subject	Work Phone	Ext.	Fax Number
6/5/2004	12:35 PM	Smith, Jane	followup call #1	(316) 554-5456	2514	

Click to close

Alphabetical Contact Listing

Contact Name	Company Name	Title	Work Phone	Ext.	Fax Num
S					
Smith, Jane			(316) 554-5456	2514	

Remember that clicking the small red "X" in any window will close it. The database saves itself with each entry, so you do not need to save it manually after creating new entries.

If you are an Access Database user, and are familiar with database creation, feel free to customize the reports and/or database fields as needed to suit your business! (Note that Mac users are unable to utilize the database.)